A Fire in Her Belly

Transforming the World, One Woman at a Time

BONNIE FATIO
FOREWORD BY MUSIMBI KANYORO

All rights reserved. Without limiting the rights under copyright reserved above, no part of this publication may be reproduced, stored in or introduced into a database and retrieval system or transmitted in any form or any means (electronic, mechanical, photocopying, recording or otherwise), in English or a translation into another language, without the prior written permission of the owner of copyright.

The people, events and information contained within this Book are strictly for educational purposes. If you wish to apply ideas contained in this Book, you are taking full responsibility for your actions. This publication is designed to provide accurate and authoritative information regarding the subject matter covered. It is sold with the understanding that the author and the publisher are not engaged in rendering legal, accounting, or other professional services. If you require legal advice or other expert assistance, you should seek the services of a competent professional.

Disclaimer: The author makes no guarantees to the results you'll achieve by reading this book. All business requires risk and hard work. The results and client case studies presented in this book represent results achieved working directly with the author. Your results may vary when undertaking any new business venture or marketing strategy.

Copyright @ 2023 Bonnie Fatio
First published 2023 Christine Robinson Global

ISBN: 978-1-7373364-2-6

Cover by optymise.co.nz & Christine Robinson

TABLE OF CONTENTS

Foreword i

Acknowledgements v

Introduction vii

What Others Have To Say xii

Chapters

1 Inspired Women Lead. 1

2 Seeds Of Inspiration 11

3 From Embassy Liaison to Following Her Dream 16

4 Overcoming The UnWorthiness Gene. 23

5 Let Me Walk In Your Shoes. 29

6 The Ripple Effect 36

7 Top Executive Discovers Self-Worth Redefines Next Chapter 44

8 A Glimpse At The Admission Process 50

9 A Vision Is Born. 54

10 The Key To A Better World 58

11 Clarity In The Tropics. 61

12 The Love And Support Of A Strong Man 69

13 From Culture Shock To Catalyst For Gender Equality 76

14 Intergenerational Guidance 82

15 Promise To Save Daughters, Saves Thousands 96

16 Corporate Partners Find Success Formula With
   Inspired Women Lead................................... 103

17 Glossophobia - The Fear Of Public Speaking.....................112

18 Authenticity Leads The Way To Personal Transformation 120

19 What's Next 127

FOREWORD

Musimbi Kanyoro

God created Bonnie Fatio to inspire women to lead without apology. I arrived at this conclusion after three decades of knowing Bonnie, meeting her and seeing her in her mentor/coach role, reading her past published and unpublished works and now by reading A Fire In Her Belly. Through her enormous certainty, articulate presence, the book draws examples from her life to inspire and motivate women to abandon their shaky confidence and take the courage to lead. Leadership is a mysterious concept with many changing interpretations. This book is not a manual on leadership but an example of leading. As it is often said. "Leadership cannot be taught. It can only be learnt."

In A Fire In Her Belly, Bonnie Fatio invites the reader to her life's journey as a daughter, a wife, mother, grandmother and a global friend to many. Besides having had a full spectrum of relational experiences, the book also reveals the life of a professional woman, a facilitator, an engaged generous volunteer and a philanthropist.

Why does this matter? It matters because our relationships shape our choices, our opportunities and even impact our behaviors. For women, it matters because our choices of leadership are often enhanced or hindered by the people in our lives. It is by sharing stories like Bonnie's, that women continue to build the collective library of possibilities from which other women can draw courage to lead. Often times, women juggle both the duties of care in the family and other capacities that invite their presence in forums beyond family. At the end of the day, leadership is about relationships which women manage all the time. Leadership effectiveness is either energized or hindered by our relationships.

What this book can do for you as a reader is to inspire you to own your leadership and just get on with it. Good leaders motivate others and Bonnie's story will motivate you to understand leadership as the power within us to contribute to making a difference and in so doing, we also become transformed. Some leaders lead institutions, organizations or government. Others volunteer for leadership roles that are needed on Boards, Councils, schools, hospitals, disaster locations, movements and the lists have no end. Bonnie realized earlier than most that she can have influence by utilizing her time, talent and treasure. She has spent uncountable volunteer hours in support of people, organizations and community. She has used her speaking skills and knowledge to influence decisions.

Bonnie's life story is also a great illustration of women's philanthropy. Traditionally donors are identified as people who visibly donate out of their public wealth. This concept excludes many donors like Bonnie Fatio. Home hosting and catering for guests is a hospitality that costs money and sometimes a lot of money. In this book, Bonnie refers to her association with International Organizations, among them, the World YWCA. These associations included hosting, not once but several times of Board members, guests and staff of the organizations. Additionally, using personal resources to travel to see these organizations in other parts of the world. And most significant, financing and hosting "Inspired Women Lead" an organization she founded. These are no mean matters and definitely count as philanthropic practice.

I know Bonnie and consider her a friend and compatriot in leadership. As I traveled along her journey in the book, I recognized many aspects that are authentic to Bonnie's leadership. Bonnie is a relational leader and knowing her means knowing her home and her family. She is a serial bridge maker who is always finding ways to connect people whose leadership might be enhanced together.

Inspiration is certainly a quality of leadership that has been recognized by many social scientists, past and present. Leaders who excel with this skill are called "inspirational leaders" and

Bonnie is definitely in this class. In addition, Bonnie has a seat among "charismatic leaders" because she stands out in her push for women's leadership. In her last publication Age Esteem, she urged women to age with grace and peace, an experience I value now and hope A Fire In Her Belly will inspire women in leadership.

Musimbi Kanyoro
March 24, 2023

This book is dedicated to
You,
the woman with a fire in her belly.

Acknowledgements

Many wonderful people surround me, encourage me, and push me further in my thinking and actions. Mentors and friends from previous generations continue to inspire me.

My loving gratitude embraces my late husband Gérard and our daughter Laetitia whose words, "You can do it" have constantly overflowed with love and practical encouragement.

I am eternally grateful to the Charter Members of Inspired Women Lead Association who believed in what I had birthed and volunteered to help develop it further: Andrea Oostenrijk, Annette Ebbinghaus, Geraldine Ang, Laetitia Fatio Gaillard, Margherita Brodbeck Roth. Each has been instrumental to IWL's growth and success.

Without my publisher Christine Robinson this book may never have seen the light. Her expertise and guidance have been invaluable and she has continuously gone the extra mile.

It was a privilege to work with Judith Halish, who interviewed, and wrote the case studies of several graduates of Inspired Women Lead (IWL). As someone exterior to IWL hearing their stories, she adroitly captured the essence of each one's fire in her belly, discoveries, and transformations.

I am thankful for the readers, who took time to review the manuscript and offer valuable feedback: Amy Balderson, Judy Filusch, Kathy Lubbers, Susan Mohney Patton, Rose Muenker, and Winny Obure.

I wish to acknowledge all the people who recognized potential within me and opened opportunities for me to grow my leadership; and to the organizations that welcomed me to share my leadership, especially ECLOF, World YWCA, American International Women's Club of Geneva, Women's International Network, Career Women's Forum, Female Wave of Change, Commission on the Status of Women, and Geneva City Council.

My gratitude extends to each IWL woman who has shared her unique leadership within IWL to assure its sustainability and the IWL alumnae who continue to transform the world, one woman at a time. Each is a role model for what "can be".

Leadership is not acquired it develops with the experiences of leading.

Bonnie Fatio

Introduction

> "The purpose of life is to live it, to taste experience to the utmost, to reach out eagerly and without fear for newer and richer experience."
> Eleanor Roosevelt

I'm Bonnie Fatio, an international speaker, author, founder of Inspired Women Lead, advocate for women and children globally, mother, grandmother, the daughter of a dad who was a Methodist minister, and of a mom who was a writer, author and teacher. I grew up in the Midwest, the second of four daughters, during segregation in the United States and before the era of women's liberation.

Thank you for choosing to read my book and helping me continue to inspire women worldwide.

This book is my legacy to you and future generations. Unlike a traditional memoir, my book is about more than my personal story. It's unique in that I share the intimate story of *Inspired Women Lead* and I also showcase other women's journeys told in their voices and perspectives. You'll get to know me as I reminisce, share stories, and ah-ha moments from my life that might spark something within you to act on your own dream.

Reading this book, you might think I was born under a lucky star, and life has been smooth. The truth is I am just like you. I have had my fair share of challenges. The difference for me is that I look at the silver lining, so I do not categorize them as challenges. Instead, my positive outlook is my lucky star, the lens through which I see the world. Even while experiencing the pain of a broken back, heart attack, temporary loss of sight, and difficulties conceiving a child, each event brought me a new understanding of who I am. They're not the focus of my life, simply opportunities that provide me with a deeper understanding and greater faith in my journey, thereby creating more exciting stories for me to share.

There's a common thread that weaves through the years for me to do more in the world. A gift that others saw in me from a young age. I see that same calling "to lead and give back" in women around the globe regardless of culture, age, or sector, and I strive to help them achieve their visions.

This book will take you on a journey through the highlights, influential people, and moments that fueled my self-discovery and quest to be a leader and change the world for the better.

You'll be amazed by the seemingly everyday little things and those once-in-a-lifetime moments when others encouraged me because they saw something special in me. From my parents to a park ranger and even Dr Martin Luther King, they each directly and profoundly shaped how I saw myself and realized my higher purpose.

In this book, I invite you to learn about Inspired Women Lead (IWL), the international women's mentoring association I created from my vision. Celebrate the personal stories of authentic feminine leaders who have enriched the organization and its program through individual experiences and successes. Hearing directly from the alumnae about their evolution will touch your heart and soul.

While I'm the founder of IWL, the association belongs to women worldwide. With a staggering 94% completion rate, the IWL program has an exponential ripple effect. The impacts on global humanity by the nearly 500 alumnae are as astonishing as the women themselves. They each prove how one woman can change the world.

My vision is outrageous, yet something most people share.

> *"I dream of a world of peace,*
> *understanding, and collaboration where*
> *each individual is valued and respected for*
> *her or his uniqueness."*

And what would that world look like?

Our children would be safe, and arms would not be necessary; health care, education, employment, and opportunities to grow in meaningful ways would be the norm for all.

I believe each woman is capable in her life of creating more peace, understanding, and collaboration, and it begins with two essential components.

> First, she needs a vision of what can be and is possible.

> Secondly, she must step into her authentic feminine leadership, regardless of where she is, doing whatever she does.

With these two steps, she will awaken each day, knowing that her presence and actions, large or minute, will have lasting effects as they build toward improving our world.

One of my favorite words in the song, Let There Be Peace on Earth, is the stanza, "let there be peace on earth and let it begin with me." Peace, understanding, and collaboration ultimately depend on the "me."

I hope that your takeaways are meaningful, inspiring, and motivate you to action. While reading my stirring anecdotes, ask yourself, 'What more can I do?'

You may discover an idea that sparks something in your life, or you may feel compelled to help someone next door or halfway around the world.

I know that one woman can change the world.

Perhaps YOU are that woman!

Bonnie Fatio

WHAT OTHERS HAVE TO SAY ...

"This book is an excellent read for any woman, no matter her age, to be inspired to learn and grow and reach inside herself."
Susan Mohney Patton

"Bonnie & I have been friends since college. It has been my pleasure following all that she has done with her life and helping women all over the world make changes in their lives. Inspired Women Lead has helped so many women internationally: working first with a mentor and then becoming one themselves. A quote from the book that embodies Bonnie's philosophy and mission so well,
 'If women felt worthy we would show up as who we are and lead with our values in such a way they would become universally accepted.' "
Judy Filusch

"If you have a grand dream but wonder how it could ever materialize, read Fire In Her Belly now! This inspiring book tells the story of how Bonnie Fatio manifested her vision of empowering women through the creation and continued expansion of Inspired Women Lead — a network of women mentoring women that uplifts, affirms and validates tens of thousands of women around the world. It shows how exponentially effective and powerful women are when they interact one-on-one, as a team and in community. "

Rose Muenker

"Leadership is taking on things that are too big for you ... that you must bring people on board to bring to fruition."

Laurence Arthur, Australia - InspiredWomen Lead 2018

"Authentic leadership removes the judgement and unburdens the mind."

Fides Nibasumba, Burundi - Inspired Women Lead 2022

"My honest wish is that we can keep the ripple effect to all women in all of our diversities everywhere in a world full of patriarchy, war and injustices, we are the spice, the inspiration and catalysts for peace, for justice, for equity and definitely a better world."

Winny Obure, Kenya – Inspired Women Lead 2020

"Having known Bonnie Fatio for over a decade and closely associated with her. To me, Bonnie, is not just a dear friend. She in fact, is an exceptional mentor, leader, and a great trainer. Bonnie can make the intergenerational connect with such ease. She is herself a towering leader, who has nurtured several young women across the globe to become successful leaders and mentors. Her dream was to build women's leadership and she founded the organization 'Inspired Women Lead' and in fact that is what the women associated with the organization do. Fruits of her labour are seeding everywhere!

I am sure the book with her experiences will be trail blazer for women to become leaders and lead the way to authentic leadership - precisely what Bonnie practices!"

Aasha Ramesh

"Bonnie Fatio's A Fire in Her Belly empowers readers to rise to their potential and provides real-world examples of women leaders overcoming adversity, all with delightful humor. Read this book and learn from one of the best."

Amy Balderson, Founder, Legacy

"Bonnie has dedicated her life to guide women from all over the world to step into their authentic feminine leadership and lead change. She has a strong vision that women can and will contribute to change.

Bonnie is a great mentor and shows women worldwide how to live life at fullest and with pizzazz."

Ingun Bol - Founder, Female Wave Of Change

"Bonnie Fatio is a radiant light of inspiration in every sense of the word… when you are seen by Bonnie you can see and become yourself more clearly, and in turn can reflect that light to allow others around you to see and become themselves more clearly. She has the beautiful gift of effortlessly grounding and joyously uplifting your soul simultaneously. I am most honored to have her as a mentor, a dear friend, and a role model of all possible goodness."

Tish Hicks

Chapter 1

Inspired Women Lead

Changing the World One Woman at a Time

2015: An idea to mentor women
2016: 10 Women, 9 Countries, 4 Continents
2023: 550 Women, 85 Countries, Every Continent

Lives Impacted: over 3 million and counting

Women are the catalyst to change the world. Globally, women are the backbone of families, shouldering the burdens and leading the way to transform their communities and countries. Yet, they struggle to garner respect or achieve the most significant influence and leadership levels.

Boys and young men learn early on that there is an expectation they will hold positions of power and authority. But unfortunately, the same is not universally true for girls and young women.

From the most rural communities in underdeveloped countries to the most advanced societies in the world, women are not yet offered the same opportunities as men.

> "Gender equality is more than a goal in itself. It is a precondition for meeting the challenge of reducing poverty, promoting sustainable development, and building good governance."
> Kofi Annan

How gender inequality manifests varies between countries, companies, and communities. Today's most significant challenge for women in leadership is to get the world to value femininity as they do masculinity. We will have parity only when women and men are represented equally in the home and at the highest levels of government and business.

It's challenging to have a global snapshot. However, if we take the example of Heads of State or Government, according to UNWomen.org, 'As of 1 January 2023, there are 31 countries where 34 women serve as Heads of State and/or Government. [1] At the current rate, gender equality in the highest positions of power will not be reached for another 130 years .'[2]

Yet there is supporting research to show that where women are part of the political decision-making process, it improves. This data is a strong indicator for more female leaders.

For example:
1. Research on panchayats (local councils) in India discovered that the number of drinking water projects in areas with women-led councils was 62 percent higher than in those with men-led councils.
2. In Norway, there's a direct causal relationship between the presence of women in municipal councils and childcare coverage. [18]

Additionally, when women hold leadership offices, governments experience other benefits which improve their people's lives. "Women demonstrate political leadership by working across party lines through parliamentary women's caucuses—even in the most politically combative environments—and by championing issues of:

- Gender equality, such as the elimination of gender-based violence
- Parental leave and childcare
- Pensions
- Gender-equality laws
- Electoral reform"

Similar to benefits seen for governments, the business sector benefits from women in senior leadership posts. In 2021, the proportion of women in senior management roles grew incrementally to 31 percent globally, the highest number ever recorded. Yet, even with this less than impressive number, women's contributions pay off with compelling results for businesses with:

- Improved financial performance
- Leveraging talent
- Reflecting the marketplace and customer perspectives
- Increased innovation

Throughout my life, I have been coaching, training, and mentoring multitudes of groups and individuals and speaking on every continent. To help more women prepare for these vital roles, in 2016 I created Inspired Women Lead (IWL), a unique peer-to-peer mentoring program where women mentor other women to develop their leadership.

My experience and heart were telling me to create a multicultural, cross-border, cross-sector, intergenerational mentoring program to bring my vision into reality. Our women-only space creates an atmosphere of safety, self-discovery, and sisterhood.

My two conditions:

1. It must be free to be available to anyone and everyone and to take the focus off money and keep it on the authentic feminine leadership of the individual.
2. It would be created with a business model different from what we see in most places so that the leadership would model the vision. I also knew that it had to be created with sustainability in mind. So it could not be about the founder; it must be about the vision.

May 2016:
Inspired Women Lead had a name, and I was interviewing the first participants from multiple countries and sectors. Some were women I had met while speaking or training; others were recommended to me by various leaders.

June 2016: the first cycle
I began mentoring ten women from nine countries: United States, Switzerland, Portugal, France, Lesotho, Malawi, India, Bangladesh, and Sri Lanka.

December 2016: the second cycle
The program's design creates cascading growth every six months. Eight of the original mentees mentored eight other women. I mentored another ten women.

Several new mentees had heard me speak in Rome at the Women's International Network (WIN) Conference, where I received the WIN Global Inspiring Women Worldwide award for "Opening new paths and improving the confidence of senior women, mentoring young ones, and bringing an innovative voice to the space of women's leadership."

Among these were corporate women seeking to widen their perspective and expand their reach beyond the companies they worked for, which included Hewlett Packard Enterprise (HPE), Microsoft, and Credit Suisse Bank.

> **"** It is a privilege to be among the first 100! **"**
> Maja Mishkarova, Macedonia

In 2022 the cycles grew to include upwards of 50-60 new women twice yearly. Now, IWL women originate from 85 countries and include entrepreneurs, community builders, journalists, movie producers, refugees, independent professionals, corporate women, healthcare workers, politicians, teachers, and more ... Each has a driving desire or what I call "a fire in their belly" to make a positive difference.

IWL's mission is to positively and sustainably transform our world by championing women globally through mentoring in authentic feminine leadership - one woman at a time.

Inspired Women Lead:
- Mentors
- Creates a catalyst for change
- Fosters Authentic Feminine Leadership
- Builds Networks· Inspires
- Builds multicultural communities

This mentoring is for the woman who is eager to be part of the program and who
- Desires to lead as her authentic feminine self
- Has a passion/dream/vision to make a positive difference in her community or beyond, although she may not be able to articulate what it is yet
- Has several years of leadership and/or professional experience and is over the age of 24
- Speaks and understands English well enough to understand concepts
- Has regular access to a dependable internet connection

I am nourished by the knowledge that for every woman I help, they'll help many others. You can see how prolific the scope of this program is by doing some simple math.

Assume for a moment that each IWL woman positively impacts only 250 people in her life, a conservative estimate to be sure. Assume those individuals are so moved that they, in turn, affect 250 people in their lives. You can see that you reach half a million and then over a hundred million in only a few iterations. The ripples are significant and extensive.

The Ripple Effect

In only 5 iterations you reach 7,910,156,250, the world's population, which at the time of writing is expected to cross the 8 Billion mark.

> " When you receive a gift like this, something this powerful and this moving, you can't keep it to yourself. There is so much abundance, learning, and knowledge in the lessons that it can't be contained to just the people in the program. It flows out into the people around you. "
>
> Wanuri Kahiu, Kenya
> Inspired Women Lead 2017

I often ask the women in the program the famous question from Marianne Williamson's book, "A Return to Love," "Who am I to be brilliant, gorgeous, talented, and fabulous? Actually, who am I not to be?"

The mentorship program within IWL is a journey of self-discovery guided by a robust training manual and strict quality measures. Each participant commits 12 months to the program. During this time, she must actively participate in one-on-one calls between mentor and mentee and in group calls led by trained alumnae from across the globe.

Ideally, new members are matched with mentors from different cultures, countries, and sectors. This inter-generational and cross-cultural approach adds depth and diversity to the experience.

Members receive mentoring in the first six months, and then the women move from being mentees to become mentors. A mentoring guide and monthly group sessions train her on the next month's theme.

> " To best assimilate what you learn, share it with someone else. "
> Bonnie Fatio

Immediately mentoring another woman within the IWL program is purposeful. It is through mentoring another woman that the mentor assimilates what she experienced as a mentee.

One aspect of the group calls builds upon the one-on-one mentoring with a series of intentional questions posed in a careful progression meant to spark deep reflection and stimulate new action. In addition, the process provides the tools to access personal milestones and discover a deeper understanding of themselves.

Exploring these questions and sharing their individual meanings across the diverse body of women gives them incredible insight and is the catalyst for remarkable personal growth for each participant.

The format encourages learning from one another through self-identification, validation, and personal stories. One guiding principle that creates a safe, judgment-free space is the unconditional acceptance of each member regardless of race, socioeconomic status, sexual orientation, age, life experience, industry, religion, or passion.

> **"** Unconditional acceptance does not mean that we must agree. It means I respect and value you as a person with unique qualities and perspectives that I can learn from. Being challenged in my opinions helps me to discover my deeper thoughts and hidden biases. It is an opportunity to learn and to perhaps modify my thoughts. **"**
>
> Bonnie Fatio

There is confidence in knowing that you are enough, your uniqueness is, in fact, your strength, and yes, you are meant to realize your dream. Therefore, we bolster women who will take the steps to positively transform their neighborhood, office, community, or beyond to benefit all people.

The IWL global movement complements initiatives already in various regions. We're not pushing anything out. Instead, the goal is to inspire authentic feminine leadership to create balance for the world to function better.

Globally, we need more women leaders who find the middle ground in compromise, propel us forward, and care for everyone regardless of status. Additionally, women are often more interested in collaboration than men.

IWL's successful mentoring program helps women emerge as authentic feminine leaders that positively transform the world and simultaneously spark the same passion in other women.

Bestowing someone with the title of "Leader" is a sign of respect, indicates significant influence within society, and transforms how the person sees herself. Being a leader is about more than being a figurehead; it's a state of mind, a presence, and a way of life.

Great leaders respect the responsibility that comes with power. Authentic Feminine Leaders are leaders in every sense of the word and exhibit qualities naturally inherent to women, such as empathy, compromise, inclusiveness, collaboration, and a more holistic perspective, to name a few.

References from: https://www.unwomen.org/en/what-we-do/leadership-and-political-participation/facts-and-figures#_edn1

[1] UN Women calculation based on information provided by Permanent Missions to the United Nations. Only elected Heads of State have been taken into account.

[2] UN Women calculations

[18] R Chattopadhyay and E Duflo (2004). "Women as policy makers: Evidence from a randomized policy experiment in India," Econometrica 72(5), pp 1409–1443; K A Bratton and L P Ray 2002. "Descriptive representation: Policy outcomes and municipal day-care coverage in Norway," American Journal of Political Science, 46(2), pp 428–437.

Chapter 2

Seeds of Inspiration

> **"** Leadership is taking on things that are too big for you ... that you must bring people on board to bring to fruition. **"** Laurence Arthur
> Australia - Inspired Women Lead 2018

How do we learn about leadership? When does leadership start? Is it taught or innate? You may be a natural-born leader, or maybe you were nurtured or forced to develop that strength. For me, it's a little of both.

Looking back, I can identify several events that encouraged my natural tendencies and reinforced what I learned at home about leadership.

One hot summer morning in 1960, I was hanging around the house with nothing special to do when my parents asked, almost as an afterthought, "Do you want to come with us? We're going to hear Dr Martin Luther King Jr speak."

My parents were eager to hear him speak, so I knew it would be a special occasion. I jumped into my summery blue and white sleeveless polka-dot dress to be presentable. I knew Dr King was the head of the civil rights movement, yet at 16 years old, that was all I knew. His speech that day was one of two Freedom Jubilee civil rights gatherings held in Pittsburgh that summer.

We drove for more than an hour, finally arriving at Forbes Field to discover the parking lot filled. So, my father dropped us off to wait while he searched for parking. It seemed an eternity. Based on how long it took him to return, he must have parked quite a distance. While we waited, many people passed by on their way to the overflowing stadium.

One gentleman even asked to take my photo. At the time, I didn't realize how much our white family must have stood out, especially me; I was tall, blonde, and with fair skin. I hadn't thought about what it would feel like to be in the minority or how welcome we would be. Everyone was polite and respectful. I felt entirely accepted, and it was beautiful.

The mood was hopeful, peaceful and full of anticipation. I will never forget being in that packed stadium that held 35,000 people. When Dr King took the stage, he was a dot at the other end of the field. When he began to speak, everything around me stopped. Dr King spoke of non-violence and acceptance, and that's precisely how the day felt to me.

Mesmerized, I focused on him, and everything around me ceased to exist. I felt – no, I knew he was speaking directly to me – he told me I had a great gift to give the world and that I must do something to make the world a better place.

My teenage self didn't know how to process this new information. First, of course, I probably told my best friend, Maggie. Beyond that, I didn't know what I could do at only 16 or what any one person could accomplish alone.

Unknowingly, that feeling and message planted inside me where it would germinate, grow, and bloom when the time was right!

I still count this memory and profound experience as a pivotal moment in my life. I will never forget the feeling and impressions of that day.

Inspired by Dr King's speech, my father took messages from the day and created several sermons to share with his parishioners. Looking back, I can only imagine the significance to my father.

Four years prior, when we lived in Wisconsin, he invited a black choir into our church even though church leaders warned against it. He knew what was right, and he went against policy and societal norms of segregation at the time.

Disciplinary actions came swiftly; within six weeks, the church board relocated our family to Pennsylvania to another church. I've discovered there's more than one type of leader. Leaders have ethical and moral responsibilities to do what's right. I learned that from my father, and I chose to follow his example.

> **"** Stand up for what you know to be right. Let your values guide you. **"**
> — Bonnie Fatio

In 2012 I heard Jesse Jackson speak in Geneva, Switzerland, at The International Club. Afterward, I introduced myself, shook his hand, and shared my experience of listening to Dr King that day in Pittsburgh, PA, all those years before. I told him that speech transformed my life. Jesse Jackson's reaction was to pull me in for a hug, a kiss on the cheek, and say, "Hold the faith."

Encounters like these might seem unusual; however, I have a long history of attracting interactions and meetings with prominent people throughout my life, be that Audrey Hepburn, a former US president, or a Princess of Thailand.

I'm sensitive to other peoples' energy and gravitate toward those who emanate positive leadership qualities.

My dad always told me, "Bonnie, you're tall; you'll stick out in a crowd one way or another, so walk tall and make it memorable."

Years later, I realized that Dr King and my father were right; I am a leader and I have a responsibility to inspire others to lead.

Giving women the skills and tools to develop and discover the leader within is a conduit to my vision of the world we all deserve.

One person can make a difference, like my father, who broke with church leaders to do what was right even at his own expense, and Dr King, who helped a country break free from segregation. We all have a gift to give the world. At some point, we each have that calling to do more.

If they did it - so can I - and if I can do it - so can YOU!

> "Today I fully affirm my role as a leader."
> Claudia Seymour
> France - Inspired Women Lead 2019

Chapter 3

From Embassy Liaison to Following Her Dream

I facilitate a group mentoring session, "Women Leading in Change," twice a year, hosted by Female Wave of Change. In 2020 my "Stepping Back – Gaining New Perspective" session was highly interactive.

One participant, Daeyoung Kim from South Korea, immediately drew my attention. Her passion for learning and fully participating, despite some reticence due to culture and language, was magnetic. When she joined Inspired Women Lead, I was delighted that I could continue to watch her leadership grow.

I know that you'll be as impressed with Daeyoung as I am.

Here's Daeyoung's story:

> Daeyoung Kim loved her work as a Public Diplomacy Specialist at the US Embassy in Seoul, South Korea for two decades. There she connected Korean opinion leaders with their counterparts from the United States (US) to maintain healthy bilateral relationships.
>
> Although at the time, women played a crucial role in Korean society, there were very few, if any, women in leadership positions.
>
> During former Secretary of State Hilary Clinton's first diplomatic trip to the region, Daeyoung was in charge of the public diplomacy segment on women's empowerment. As the pioneer of the South Korean women's empowerment portfolio, it was a tremendous honor for her and her family.
>
> Despite the gratifying work, Daeyoung says, "I woke up one day and felt I wanted to do more, something bigger." She yearned to expand her reach beyond the US and Korea. She knew she wanted to help women and young people discover their leadership potential and the impact they could spark in a global society.
>
> Her career required focus, and splitting her attention to anything new would be unfair.
>
> So, without an actual plan, Daeyoung decided to make a change; leaving the Embassy position behind, she began to pursue her new calling.

Over the next few years, she took various leadership trainings offered by several international organizations building her skills and meeting women from around the world through virtual conferences and classes. In addition, Daeyoung also trained as an Emotional Intelligence (EQ) practitioner.

Late in 2020, she joined other international women to participate in a group mentoring session led by Bonnie Fatio. So impressed by Bonnie and Inspired Women Lead (IWL), she immediately emailed Bonnie to express her desire to join the mentoring program.

"The IWL program is a revolutionary journey," Daeyoung says. The program and the topics addressed in every cycle are consistent. Yet, each woman's life experiences dramatically impact how she receives the information, expresses herself during the program, and eventually shows up in the world. So, while the questions are the same from person to person, no two answers are identical.

"These discoveries helped me become confident in myself and paved the way for my career," Daeyoung says.

Prior to IWL, Daeyoung was fortunate to receive guidance from world leaders and great thinkers. However, she did not have the time to delve deeper into their meaning. That piece came from the structure of the IWL program.

IWL creates unexpected pairings between mentors and mentees. For example, Daeyoung's much younger mentor was a French scientist married with two children, living and working in Australia.

Initially, Daeyoung was surprised that her mentor differed from herself in age, industry, life experience, and country. Yet, they quickly developed a close connection sharing many personal stories and core values.

The program's structure allows 45 minutes of one-on-one attention to the mentee at each session. This luxury of focused time is imperative to the individual's development. "The time and caring I received is beyond words or monetary value," Daeyoung says.

Daeyoung recognizes the incredible feeling of being surrounded by safety and acceptance. Generosity comes from the heart, and everyone in the program gives this way. From cycle to cycle, the receiver then becomes the giver. It creates an endless chain of empathy.

When it came time for Daeyoung to be the mentor, she was scared that she had nothing to offer. However, she appreciated the monthly training that supported her role as a mentor.

In hindsight, she says, "I did not need to be afraid. IWL taught me how to use the guidebook as a reference tool effectively. It's quite fundamental. The manual is full of wisdom. It's a simple approach to a deeply personal and professionally beneficial journey."

Recognizing that people are a little nervous when faced with new responsibilities, Daeyoung happily shares her initial feelings of trepidation to help ease others' concerns.

Daeyoung's mentee was a Spanish woman living and working in Switzerland with her family. As a legal expert, the mentee worked for a demanding, high-pressure start-up while simultaneously trying to create a work-life balance. As a result, she's very logic-based, whereas Daeyoung comes more from a heart-centered approach.

The mentee shared that she thought she would have to sacrifice having children for a career early on. Then she noticed a female colleague who was both professionally successful and had three children. She thought, "If she can, I can!" That simple phrase also touched something deep within Daeyoung.

For Daeyoung, this issue brought up feelings around "imposter syndrome" and self-guilt. She felt she could be a better person and do more. Daeyoung says Korean society judges women as "selfish" for even expressing a yearning to take time for self-care. So it's no wonder she felt guilty.

The mentoring phase is equally as beneficial as the mentee portion, both offering growth.

IWL's training provided Daeyoung with the tools to help others uncover their inner leader. Upon completing the program in 2022, she envisioned how to support and assist others in their self-discovery process.

She says the program is for anyone willing to listen and serve. It's not about teaching or giving someone all the answers. Instead, it's about being in the moment and giving genuine empathy.

Leaving the security of her colleagues and friends at the embassy, she felt lost. Happily, IWL's training gave her a new sense of belonging and greater independence.

While many organizations now feel like home, she doesn't need external validation to know her worth. She knows she is enough and that she belongs everywhere.

Daeyoung is the founder and CEO of IMI Partners, Inc., which provides Emotional Intelligence workshops and instruction to companies, non-governmental organizations (NGOs), and educators to use their emotions and intelligence to make good choices.

On a larger scale, she's expanded her role from embassy liaison between two countries to now being the bridge that connects her fellow Koreans to many cultures.

Daeyoung urges any woman looking for her unique gifts or noble causes to apply for the Inspired Women Lead program. As an Alumna, she recognizes this potential in other women she meets globally and introduces them to the program's benefits. Referrals are an expression of her gratitude and help ensure the longevity of the IWL program.

"I owe them who I am today. I'm no longer afraid to be alone because I belong everywhere," Daeyoung says.

Chapter 4

Overcoming The ~~Un~~Worthiness Gene

For years, as I traveled around the world, I looked for opportunities to engage women in conversations. My questions often dealt with aging or women's leadership.

Long before the inception of Inspired Women Lead, while speaking and training in countries such as Bangladesh, Nepal, Myanmar, China, Japan, Colombia, Kenya, Uganda, South Africa, Canada, Germany, France, Spain, Ireland, and Scotland, I began a dialogue about what the real issues were for women.

What I found to be the most universally shared emotion among women is what they call a lack of confidence. However, as one digs deeper, it becomes clear that it is much more than a simple lack of confidence.

It seems that as women, we do not believe ourselves worthy, as though we were born with a gene labeled "unworthiness." This unworthiness stands in our way of showing up as authentic feminine leaders.

It's no surprise since we have been bathed and dressed in this belief for generations. Indeed, I have had to fight my feelings of inadequacy and thoughts that others were more deserving of using their voice. I did not recognize my value.

I've asked several female world leaders, "Do you believe this is common to all women to some degree?" Consistently the answer has been "yes." Even Her Eminence Julia Gillard, former Prime Minister of Australia, stated this was true. This outspoken, dynamic politician also admitted that it applied to her. To me, her admission takes great courage and vulnerability.

Is this gene so strong because women were the property of men for so many generations? If we are honest, women are still the property of men in many, perhaps even most, parts of the world.

Look around; even in very progressive countries, we constantly see women ruled by men making decisions for them. The decisions made about us by men make us their property, just as if "property of..." were tattooed on us. Is it in our DNA?

It certainly does not give us the impression that we merit an opportunity to make our own decisions, be it about our own bodies, our right to education, to work, to move freely, to hold office, and most importantly, our right to show up as our authentic feminine selves.

So when I speak about the "Unworthiness Gene," it is not a cute title; it is the prevalent issue among women worldwide. It's as though we "know" we are not worthy; we do not merit equal pay, a place at the table, a voice on the board, and, depending on the culture, the right to a bank account, property ownership, and control over our own bodies.

The title of my speech, "Unworthiness Gene," has a strikethrough line across "Un" because it is time to create a "Worthiness Gene" for women. Scientists are now saying we can change our DNA within our lifetime. It is exciting to imagine what this might mean for us as we genuinely transform it into a worthiness gene!

One tip to help you overcome the feeling of unworthiness is to admit you are not worthy and then prove yourself wrong. In my own life, the most effective remedy has been to stretch myself beyond my comfort in some small or not-so-small way daily.

When you do this, you are constantly growing, expanding yourself in new ways until it becomes a way of life. You don't even notice it's happening until one morning you wake up and find yourself acting as if you are worthy in a situation that would have left you trembling just months before.

This next story illustrates how in one moment, everything changes when you realize that you are worthy and have been all along.

Due to happy circumstances Kofi Annan, former Secretary General of the United Nations, and his wife Nane became very dear friends. Invited to his 75th birthday, I was seated next to a former president, which indicated my hosts held me in similar esteem. Kofi and Nane did not question my "worthiness"; I did. Feeling I wasn't their equal, I waited for someone else to introduce me to guests during the reception preceding dinner.

I realized that my unworthiness was in high gear that night, as it caused me to think, who was I to be mingling with these heads of state? But of course, that was before I founded Inspired Women Lead, which has been as transforming for me as it has for the participants.

> "Every time I work with women who live in different cultures and countries, I feel inspired by my own leadership. We each constantly learn and grow in our leadership when we open our hearts and minds to each other."
>
> Bonnie Fatio

Five years later, we attended Kofi Annan's 80th birthday. The first portion of the evening was at Kofi's alma mater, the prestigious Graduate Institute of International and Development Studies in Geneva, where he was interviewed for the BBC's HARDtalk program.[25] The auditorium overflowed with interested public and guests. My husband Gérard and I were invited to the private party which followed, at the World Meteorological Organization with a breathtaking view of Geneva from the top floor, well worth the 5-minute stroll.

I saw Mary Robinson, former president of Ireland and former High Commissioner of Human Rights, walking in front of us. Unlike the previous party, I asked my husband to hurry up so I could introduce them to each other since they were both actively advocating renewable energies.

Without hesitation, I reminded her who I was, having met several times and been on the same panel years before at a World YWCA conference. Then, I introduced her to Gérard, and I continued to introduce myself to other world leaders throughout the evening.

The difference between the party five years earlier and this one was that I now saw myself as a peer to others. I was worthy. My entire life, I was brought up to know that I was a leader with a gift to make the world a better place. Yet, somehow, at Kofi's first party, I felt unworthy, like an imposter.

There's a difference between impostor syndrome or unworthiness and showing up as your authentic feminine self with an inner confidence that can only come through knowing, "I am worthy."

At the second event, I was different. Some might say, more confident, when in reality, I simply allowed my authentic feminine self to lead the way. As my father said all those years ago, "Bonnie, you're tall - one way or another, people will remember you, so make it good."

If women felt worthy, we would show up as who we are and lead with our values in such a way that they would become universally accepted.

What a relief it would be if we all showed up as our true selves. Interactions between women and men would be more natural and easier, opening the door for both sexes to live authentically. People could all finally stop pretending to be someone they aren't and don't want to be.

While women have made significant progress toward this vision, we still have a long way to go before it's a reality. Nevertheless, I believe the path will be fun yet require courage and authentic leadership as the model to forge ahead.

In 2023 we still do not support each other as sisters unconditionally, nor do we necessarily recognize our inherent value to each other. Who else can understand me better than a woman who has walked in her own shoes on similar paths? What man knows what it is like to menstruate or give birth?

There are so many ways that we understand each other as women if we allow ourselves to celebrate who we are as a feminine tribe and join forces to create a better world.

---

[25] https://www.graduateinstitute.ch/news-events/news/kofi-annan-calls-cool-heads-syria

Chapter 5

Let me walk in your shoes ...

Sometimes you need to walk in another woman's shoes to know her. I've accomplished much in my life, yet my trip to Uganda was life-changing. It was the 1990s and well before Inspired Women Lead came to life.

I say yes to as many opportunities as possible, as I have had the most incredible encounters and experiences. I believe everything up to this point had prepared me to become a board member of the Ecumenical Church Loan Fund (ECLOF).

My work history ranges from starting my own businesses to education, healthcare, management, coaching, and advising leaders. Yet what I did on the side was far more interesting than my career.

I served as:

- President of the American Women's Club of Geneva (1,400 members from 52 countries)
- President of the Parent's Associations for eight collèges (the high schools of Geneva)
- Elected City Councilor of the City of Geneva
- Global Ambassador of Women's Leadership of the World YWCA
- Global Ambassador of Female Wave of Change (FWOC)

And on the:

- Taskforce at the United Nations, seeking equal opportunities for women
- Advisory Council of local leaders to the High Commissioner for Refugees, Mrs Ogata
- Board of the Ecumenical Church Loan Fund (ECLOF)

Serving on the board of ECLOF was a unique privilege and my first global experience. ECLOF is the predecessor of today's microcredit programs. In 1946 following the Second World War, a private Swiss banker and the first Secretary General of the World Council of Churches created ECLOF. Funding came from church donations and a John D. Rockefeller, Jr. endowment.

ECLOF extended credit to European churches to restore and repair extensive damage from the bombings. The churches repaid the initial loans with interest, and donations continued to roll in.

When I joined in the 1990s, ECLOF International operated in over 60 developing countries. Serving during this period was exciting. First, the organization's internal culture shifted from a grant-dependency model to self-sustainability. Second, with more women on the board and a unified voice, women were finally allotted 50% of all project funding.

I had the incredible honor of being part of two ECLOF regional conferences. We toured projects in the Philippines, Kenya, and Uganda. My experiences were extraordinary. The local women working at the grassroots level were the epitome of authentic feminine leadership. I left my heart in Uganda and Kenya.

Ask me exactly where I was in any of these countries; I honestly couldn't tell you. It was before GPS and cell phones, yet that didn't bother me. I have an appetite for adventure and faith in my purpose.

Heifers Provide a Bright Future

Our delegation to Uganda traveled into the countryside to meet the grant recipients. To reach the villages, we rode on a school bus missing half of its floor. We felt every bump bouncing along the rough roads, and the dust billowed through the holes. I cracked my head more than once. Some might complain about the conditions; however, I loved every moment of this incredible journey.

We headed to a village, or so I thought. When the bus halted at the first stop, we scanned the horizon for signs of human life. There was nothing to see except a barren hill though looks can be deceiving. Our group sat wondering if we were in the wrong place. Finally, sensing our confusion and growing concern, our guide said, "It's okay, just wait."

Reluctantly, we all piled out of the bus and waited in anticipation. The only sounds came from nature. Suddenly, we heard music coming over the hillside. Before long, the people from the surrounding areas flooded over the hill towards us. These joyous people honored us with their traditional welcome of singing and dancing. The colorful dresses and headwraps melded with the African music and movements bringing chills of excitement despite the torrid heat, and we found ourselves moving to the rhythm with them.

We divided into smaller groups and paired up with locals. As we set out for the day, my contingent was five ECLOF delegates and seven local women who had received credit loans.

The Uganda project was a partnership with Heifer International, which granted each of them a cow. The women invited us to meet their precious cows. The locals revere cows and livestock because they provide many benefits to families, from food to income.

By the time we walked about 20 meters (approximately 65 feet), two male delegates had already turned around. They headed back to the bus stating it was too far to walk. The remaining delegates turned around when the bus was out of sight.

Not me! I respected these women, so I continued. As the only remaining delegate, I would not disappoint or disrespect them. History has taught me that women can rely on other women.

Communication was a challenge since none of us spoke a common language. Nevertheless, women are creative, and we relied on a modified form of sign language to bridge the gap.

Because I took a leap of faith, I spent this sacred time with these seven women visiting their farms. Calling these properties farms was generous, still, they were grateful for what they had.

Throughout the day, I learned that the cow represented hope, education for their children, and a better life. They produce food for the family, and extra milk and butter equates to income. If they are lucky enough to get a calf, it's the next generation and signifies longevity and sustainability. Their stories were rich, authentic, and inspiring. I was flattered to have a front-row seat.

These women had tremendous pride in their farms and their cows. They were the ones who were saving their families and improving their conditions. While technically not the leaders of their villages, these women demonstrated authentic feminine leadership.

I had my picture taken with seven different cows — one at each little farm.

From Stranger to Sisters

Even though it was getting dark when we headed towards the last farm, my guides wanted me to see every cow. So, making gestures with my hands, I joked, "You're taking me back to the bus later, right?" They all laughed and said, "Yes, yes," and they assured me they would escort me to the bus.

When we finished at the last farm, night had fallen over us like a cloak, and there was no moon. It was so dark that I couldn't see my feet, much less the trail or my companions. Yet, not knowing where I was, without the benefits of GPS or light from a mobile phone, and being utterly dependent on these women, I knew they'd ensure my safe return. Moreover, I felt an intense caring and love emanating from them; it was palpable even in the obscure night.

Here's a beautiful demonstration of trust, confidence, and transcendent communication. The women knew the route we walked so well that they guided me safely and silently in total darkness. An invisible yet gentle hand would maneuver my head down or lift my foot to avoid branches overhead and roots or rocks below my feet. Despite the lack of light and rough terrain, I never stumbled.

Arriving back at the bus unscathed, I thought about how transformational the day had been. When our delegation arrived, the villagers viewed us as god-like and me as the embodiment of a 'rich, white, European woman'. It bothered me because I always see and treat people as my equals. I felt no superiority toward them.

At the beginning of the day, they saw me as from another world, yet we connected at a heart level through our shared experiences and mutual respect and need for each other. By the end of the day, we were sisters.

We bonded for life. I still carry them with me today, and their love and kindness toward me flow out to everyone else I meet.

The phrase, "to give is to receive" is an absolute truth. When I give of myself, I experience what I can only describe as bliss in my soul.

By giving my time, energy, and respect, I transformed by meeting and walking with the women of Uganda into the dead of night to meet their cows. I had that same feeling climbing out of the ravine with the women of Kenya. (I'll share this amazing story later.)

Chapter 6

The Ripple Effect

It's incredible to be part of something greater than myself, and to serve others. Each time I witness the joy of female grant recipients worldwide, I swell with the same level of pleasure, knowing there is hope for the world.

Participating with ECLOF to improve water accessibility in Africa left me with a lasting impression. Since then, I haven't consumed or thought about water in the same way.

Globally, ECLOF works with those in the poorest socioeconomic conditions. For example, less than 10% of rural Africa's wealthiest people have on-site water access, and more than sixty percent of the poorest must gather water from unimproved sources.

According to the UN in 2021, "There's a direct correlation between water access, endemic poverty, and food insecurity. One in three Africans face water scarcity." [27]

Mount Kenya is the second-highest peak in Africa, second only to Kilimanjaro. Getting water to these marginalized areas is challenging. Females perform the hazardous and grueling task of fetching water. Often, the water they carry weighs as much as a baby hippopotamus (50kg or 110lbs). Astonishingly, they do it on their heads.

At the time of my visit, "the process of retrieving water could take women up to 8 hours daily, traveling approximately 6 kilometers (3.7 miles) multiple times a day." [30]

Women leave their villages early in the morning and often walk barefoot, along dusty dirt roads and rugged paths, which only take the women so far. Once the trail ends, they descend into the ravine using make-shift ladders from weak tree trunks and small branches. Then while balancing the weight of the water containers, they navigate the remaining journey. After they collect the water, they reverse the process to climb back.

Consider one liter of water weighs 1 kilogram, and 1 gallon of water weighs 8 pounds. The average person living in rural Kenya uses approximately 30 liters daily. Carrying that much weight multiplied over the needs of a village is daunting.

Imagine living in the United Kingdom or the United States and having to haul your water. Water usage in the "United Kingdom and the United States is 334 liters and 578 liters per person per day, respectively." [31]

Bonnie and the women of Mount Kenya - 1996

This ECLOF grant funded a pipeline to draw the water up from the bottom of the ravine. I gladly accepted the invitation to attend the dedication ceremony for the pipeline.

The locals often lay out food to welcome us whenever we arrive in an area. While enjoying the gracious refreshments, we were abruptly surrounded by men in jeeps and told they would drive us down to the water site - **now**. Excited to show us around, the chiefs and other men leapt into the vehicles.

Immediately, I realized something wasn't right. So, I asked another delegate from ECLOF, "Do you see something wrong with this picture?" The local women stood motionless, and I gathered it was because the men didn't invite them.

We decided I would take care of the situation. I signaled the women to join us; "You must come with me. After all, you made this happen." We crammed 12 people into a space meant for six. There was an elbow in my ear and a knee in someone's eye; we didn't think we'd survive the trip. We arrived safely, though everyone was shaken.

The goal was to get to the water source for the dedication ceremony, so I was stunned when the jeeps stopped quite a distance from the destination. From there, we walked, well, more accurately, we climbed into the ravine. This experience gave us a glimpse of what these resilient women endured for generations.

A Perilous Cliffside Adventure

After the ceremony, I commented on the pipe by asking the women, "Is that the pipe?" I should have left it alone when they replied, "Yes." Instead, I clarified by asking, "Does it bring the water directly to the top?"

They thought I wanted to see the entire length of the pipeline when in reality, I was merely expressing curiosity.

Perhaps the misunderstanding was part language gap, mixed with the day's excitement and the immense gratitude of the women, but suddenly we were climbing up the sheer cliffside. The local men were unhappy with me and took the easier way back to the top.

Let me be clear, this wasn't suitable for climbing, nor was it a mountainside. It was soil, gravel, and tiny root ends sticking out of the cliff. We would have been thrilled for a solid stone mountain upon which to hold.

There were 24 of us, eight from our delegation and 16 local women. When I'm asked how long we climbed, I can say, "I counted seconds, not minutes, because we could have died at any moment. It was a heart-stopping experience."

Unlike the usual route to the water, this climb didn't have any precarious ladders made of roots; that would have been a luxury. Instead, the women helped each of us hold onto the dirt. It was perilous.

One woman was guiding me from the front and another from behind. They would position my foot and place it while I held on for dear life, gripping a twig or tiny rock outcropping. Anywhere along the way, the dirt could have crumbled in our hands. I tried not to look below, but glancing way down, I could see the water in the ravine waiting for a misstep to swallow us up.

It's beyond me how the local women successfully guided us to the top. I still don't know how I or the other delegates did it. I prayed hard and put my faith in these women.

Back on solid ground, everyone celebrated that we had made it alive. Knowing I was the instigator, my colleagues considered pushing me back over the edge. Thankfully, instead, we united and created a deep connection by surviving that harrowing climb together.

Once my heart started again and my breathing normalized, I became acutely aware that I could have been responsible for the death of everyone that day.

Can you even begin to imagine these women, and generations before, climbing the ravine while carrying the village's water?

Easing water access improved these women's lives significantly. In contrast to the men, the women were so grateful that they were willing to rock climb with bare hands and feet as their only gear to demonstrate the depth of their appreciation.

I greatly respect women around the world who strive for something better. They're the heavy lifters of their villages. I've seen it repeatedly; women are the backbone of their communities. They put food in bellies and often lead in unique and undervalued ways in their cultures.

The Mount Kenya women envisioned enriching their community by making water more accessible. I often wonder how their visions have shifted now that they've realized one aspect.

Visions are enormous; they're not one and done. Mine is continually expanding. When I think I'm close to achieving it, my vision extends further than I can imagine. It tugs at me, pulling me forward, and there's always more to do.

My time with ECLOF and the women from these villages was one piece of my vision. When I accepted the board position, I had no clue that I would receive so much fulfillment, and it fueled my desire to continue to do good in the world.

I do not pretend to be able to walk their path. However, I do have tremendous empathy for what the women experience.

As leaders, we need to consider our decision's effect on others. There's a nuance that occurs in authentic leadership development that benefits everyone. While we are trailblazers and risk-takers, we ought to know when to be out front and when to guide from behind.

There are times when we share leadership. In one instance, we are ahead, another when we are shoulder-to-shoulder with our teams or followers, and in other situations, we step back and allow them to find their strength.

I may have started the day as a leader, yet by the end, the women stepped forward to lead us. We smartly deferred to their expertise. Without them, we might not have survived.

If you're wondering, the local men awaited our return with iced cold colas.

Just like in Uganda, the women of Mount Kenya saved and forever altered my life. You don't have to climb an African ravine to realize what an impact a shared experience can have.

Whether you start in your community or reach beyond, find ways where you can get involved to make a difference. I promise you that everyone will receive unexpected gifts.

---

[27] https://www.brookings.edu/blog/africa-in-focus/2021/07/23/addressing-africas-extreme-water-insecurity/

Chapter 7

Top Executive Discovers Self-Worth Redefines Next Chapter

Founded in 1997 by the renowned thought leader Kristin Engvig, WIN is a global network dedicated to empowering and connecting women leaders in work communities.

In 2017 I made many connections at the WIN Conference in Oslo, Norway. Unfortunately, I don't specifically remember the moment I met Renée, although I recently saw a photo of the two of us there. However, I clearly remember interviewing her as part of the application process to Inspired Women Lead and thinking she would be a wonderful addition to the IWL Executive Council. This role would have to wait, though, since there's a prerequisite that every council member must complete the 12-month program.

Having just left her corporate position, Renée was eager to

become involved in supporting women more meaningfully. So, I introduced her to Female Wave of Change (FWoC), which welcomed her with a board position.

You might find it unusual that I would recommend Renée to another association. However, a distinctive aspect of authentic feminine leadership is that we help other women reach their potential, even if we might lose them to another organization. For authentic women leaders, there is no competition, only collaboration.

Here is Renée's story:

> After more than 30 years in the Global Technology field as a Human Resource leader, Renée returned home to the Netherlands. Her latest assignment had been a five-year stretch in Singapore. Then, during a corporate merger, she took the opportunity to leave the company and give herself time to think about what she wanted next.
>
> Leaving corporate life behind meant letting go of the executive title, company car, air miles, and expense accounts while simultaneously redefining her individual worth. "I needed to revisit my identity and ask myself what I wanted to do with the rest of my life," Renee says.
>
> She was almost always the only woman on the leadership team. Renée said that brought her success and good fortune, although sometimes frustration. So, as she reflected on this disparity, the seed of an

idea was planted. Maybe she could leverage her experience to help other women in leadership roles reach the upper levels of companies.

Following a hunch, Renée attended the 2017 conference in Norway hosted by WIN. She went intending to get input and ideas for her current career question and to enjoy the company of other successful women.

Renée met an inspiring woman named Bonnie Fatio at the conference. While the two didn't talk all that long, Renee learned of Bonnie's vision and was intrigued. The seed began to grow within Renée.

It wasn't long before she joined Bonnie's Inspired Women Lead program. IWL provided Renée with a safe space to explore without judgment. The support and acceptance from the group reminded her of her many strengths and accomplishments. It bolstered her confidence and reframed her successes.

The program's design creates ample space and time to reflect and deeply explore each woman's values around specific topics. "That was really impactful because I had to think about these things, even if it was difficult. I was rethinking my life and reshaping the next ten years," says Renée.

Through her experiences as a mentee and a mentor, she discovered that women have much more in common than they are different. IWL's unique approach that matches seemingly dissimilar women validates this lesson. When matched with someone from a different country, different professional area, and different life phase, she quickly learned that these differences vanished. Instead, their similar mindsets helped to create a strong bond between them.

"When you come from a good place with intentions to help another, your support has a tremendous impact. In my case, I felt my mentor's pure desire to help, and I offered the same to my mentee."

Of the IWL program, Renée says she 'let go and let it happen'. She discovered she could "define a new future, plan, and vision at any time." It could evolve as she evolved.

Prioritizing life balance was finally valuable to her. However, without IWL, she wouldn't have dedicated the time to discover what it meant or how to achieve it.

Armed with this new outlook, she had a much clearer view of what she could offer others with confidence. So, she divided her time between her new coaching and mentoring business, Capricorn HR Consulting, and volunteering with a few organizations that empower women to create change.

For IWL, Renée volunteered to apply her exceptional organizational skills first to their application process and other aspects of the association. In addition, she lent her leadership to the monthly mentor training calls, helping to support and develop each cycle of new mentors.

Renée was influential in reviewing and updating the interviewing guide lending her years of experience to help streamline processes and consistency. Her input helped improve the overall quality that IWL is known to provide.

Currently, she is a member of the IWL Executive Council, responsible for the application and onboarding of new members, matching mentor-mentee pairs, and recruiting and training volunteers from the pool of Alumnae.

Having reinforced her 'unconditional acceptance' of others, Renée is more open to connecting with people outside her accustomed circle and understanding different perspectives.

Influenced by the concept of being authentic as a leader, Renée has the words to express her values and leads from that space.

While Renée is still busy, it's different than when she was a corporate executive. Now she's doing what she loves and has time to enjoy her life. Surprisingly, she's found something she didn't know she was missing, a life-work balance.

Renée's advice: "If you are thinking about a change, have an idea or feeling that you're called to do more, or if you want to improve who you are as a leader and you have the time to devote to it – Do it!"

Renée says, "In general, women have unique qualities, and when they are equipped and encouraged to use their strengths and energies confidently, the world will be better off and, overall, more compassionate."

"In IWL, we accept, value, and respect everyone – the world needs more of that now more than ever," says Renée.

Chapter 8

A Glimpse of the Admission Process

As you can see from Renée's story, IWL has dramatically benefited from her expertise in organization and creating systems, and Renée has found her way to change the world.

When Renee joined the IWL Executive Council (EC), she took over Onboarding and Engagement. She worked closely with EC member Andrea Oostenrijk, responsible for IT, who introduced technical systems and support to streamline processes further. These enhancements upgraded our application and interviewing processes while preserving mentees and mentors at the heart of the experience.

I consider it a great tribute to the effectiveness of our mentoring that Alumnae and participants nominate many of our future applicants. We accept applications anytime, and the interview process occurs bi-annually during the two months preceding the start of the mentoring programs in spring and fall. Women aspiring to be in our program first complete the online application. Next is a virtual interview with one of the Executive Council members, who ultimately determines which candidates best fit the program.

As always, we look for women with a fire in their bellies. You might be wondering, what exactly does that mean?

It means she has a vision and is looking to be of higher service to others in her organization, community, or beyond. She is not satisfied with some aspects of the world, which drives her first to make changes in herself as she prepares to step into her vision.

So, we identify which women have the right spirit and motivation and the availability and dedication for the time commitment. She must also demonstrate leadership experience and explain why she wants to join IWL.

Of course, diversity is paramount; I want women to realize that we are much more alike than we are different. That realization starts the ripple of effective change we need in the world. So, we also match the mentor and mentee pairs to be as dissimilar as possible.

We precisely match mentors with mentees in hopes that each will learn from the other. For instance, we will match a shy woman with a mentor who will create an exceptionally safe environment to assist the mentee in opening up and finding her voice. Similarly, if the mentee is most comfortable in her head, we choose someone to help her get in touch with her heart.

Trained Pair Guides also assist in the process. They are Alumnae who volunteer to support the mentor-mentee pairs. Having more experience, they encourage and provide feedback and suggestions, ensuring all participants are successful in the program.

The Executive Council and Alumnae support the active pairs to ensure they're on track, participating in the calls, and providing the tools and space necessary to complete the program.

It's also worthy of note that women-only spaces are as important today for developing female leaders as at any time in history.

Zoe Fenson writes in *The Week: Why Women-Only Spaces Still Matter,* "Women-only spaces offer a respite from the pressure — and often, trauma — wrought by social conditioning. When a man enters a room full of women, his experiences and viewpoints immediately define the conversation. Unconsciously and instinctively, the women in the room step back. They moderate their words. They watch for signs of his discomfort and rush to soothe hurt feelings." [33]

Some might disagree with this statement; however, Daeyoung recently shared something she witnessed in a meeting between a US diplomat and Korean business people. While the diplomat spoke with a female manager, the male staff members felt no hesitation to interrupt the conversation. Then, feeling compelled to make room for the men, the female boss stepped back, allowing this disrespect.

This behavior is not just a South Korean cultural issue. It happens globally every day because it's part of generations of conditioning.

Because of this conditioning, coed management training and mentoring aren't as beneficial for women as non-coed ones. As a result women thrive in women-only spaces, and we try things we wouldn't do in front of men because we allow ourselves to be vulnerable once safe from judgment, expectations, ramifications, or retaliation.

Women encourage other women to be themselves, show up authentically, and discover that they're enough and don't have to be like men to succeed. Women understand, respect, and validate our experiences in ways men cannot. As a result, IWL Alumnae go forward with a new level of confidence, clarity, authenticity, communication, and authentic leadership, which also means that their visions become more accessible.

---

[33] https://theweek.com/articles/817555/why-womenonly-spaces-still-matter

Chapter 9

A Vision is Born

> " Step into your dream.
> Live it. Feel it. Smell it. Taste it. Touch it.
> Hear it. See it. Experience it.
> - It is no longer a dream. "
>
> Bonnie Fatio

Almost everyone says they have a vision, a vision board, or some mission they want to accomplish. Yet, not everyone takes the next step. So, my best advice, follow through even if you're unsure. There's always someone like me to help you.

No matter how wispy it is, a vision is fundamental to bringing positive change to the world. A vision isn't a goal; it's much more significant and has the potential to affect change around the world. It's a burning desire that gnaws at you repeatedly.

The volunteer time I spent under the umbrella of the World YWCA as their Global Ambassador of Women's Leadership was a privilege. It was during this time that the idea of Inspired Women Lead first sparked within me.

I didn't suddenly become a global ambassador. My relationship with the World YWCA began when the Secretary General, Dr Musimbi Kanyoro, asked me to provide a training segment at their International Training Institute. Women from 52 different cultures came with eager minds and open hearts.

I gave them an exercise where each woman was given a piece of A4 paper and asked to figure out how she could pull her body through it from feet to head. She could cut or tear the paper while keeping the four sides intact. Before that day, I had only seen it done one way.

These incredible women came up with three ways to successfully achieve the goal. When there's no judgment or rules, all solutions are free to emerge. I want women everywhere to do the same and find their own out-of-the-box solution for all of life's puzzles or challenges.

Watching each woman approach and solve the puzzle was beautiful. Following the training, the women celebrated with diverse cultural enthusiastic appreciation. One woman stood on a table stomping her feet; others used their hands to clap or drum the table, and some used vocal sounds. The women conveyed their feelings in a universal expression of joy.

That day every woman discovered something about herself, and I was no exception. It is from sharing what I knew with others that I gained even more. I found a calling to be part of the World YWCA.

I knew that I had to do something more. So afterwards, I told Secretary General Dr Musimbi Kanyoro, "As of this moment, you have a month of my professional time yearly. Just tell me how you want to use it." From there, my honorary role eventually grew into being the Global Ambassador for Women's Leadership. Making that commitment was one of the greatest gifts I could offer myself.

> "Encouraging another woman to step into her leadership is a first step toward positively transforming society."
>
> Bonnie Fatio

I helped train women in exotic locations such as Colombia, Nepal, Bangladesh, Thailand, Myanmar, and African countries and more traveled destinations such as Europe and North America. I also helped create Intergenerational Transformative Leadership, a co-teaching concept where women of different generations share the stage and teach together.

Even now, I have moments when I first take the stage alone where I miss the magic that happens for the audience and the speakers when two or more women of different generations collaborate for the benefit of others.

As I reflect, I am vividly aware that no matter how much I give of my time and talents, I receive oh so much more. Every experience is full of examples of ways I receive. They can be intangible, like the feeling of joy at the YWCA training exercise, gratitude for the women of Uganda, and developing more courage and trust to climb a cliff in Kenya.

I give solely with the desire to improve another woman's life, which opens me up to grow from shared experiences.

I invite you to ask yourself, "What have I unexpectedly received while giving to others?"

Chapter 10

The Key To A Better World...

During my time with the world YWCA, I focused on leadership, and my vision grew organically. Without those experiences, who knows when or if IWL would have become a reality. I don't want to think of one life, let alone the millions of lives, untouched if I hadn't created IWL. For this and so many other reasons, the World YWCA was the most influential component in my growth.

My entire life seems to have involved speaking with women and women's groups, leading organizations with a female-dominant presence, and coaching or mentoring women working toward greater roles in management, education, or government. Then, it was as though I woke up one day, knowing I was meant to create something like IWL. And that, in various iterations,

I'd been doing it all along because that's where I gravitated; it attracted me. This has been true for me and is probably true for you too.

While the Intergenerational Transformative Leadership program helps women of different generations respect, support, and collaborate, my AgeEsteem book motivates and challenges women to reach new heights as we age. Both are independent of each other and created at different points in my life, yet naturally in alignment with who I am and what I believe.

Remember, IWL was still an idea deep within me while leading within the YWCA. Be gentle with yourself; your vision may still be marinating.

Like you, I'm constantly growing. For instance, when I mentored a new church pastor, we had a dialogue where I shared that I felt I was here to do more. He was surprised because, from his perspective, I was already doing it. I shared that what I was doing with AgeEsteem was a steppingstone toward something greater. There was still a nagging inside me, a little voice saying, "You're meant to do more."

Like me and every woman I've met, you also have something greater you want to do, even if you don't know what it is.

All I have accomplished in my life is due to the many people who have encouraged and believed in me. One, in particular, was the General Secretary to the World YWCA, Dr Musimbi Kanyoro, an extraordinary woman who most recently was the CEO/President of the Global Fund for Women. Among her most important titles for those of us who know her are: role model, mentor, and dear friend.

I love when women celebrate together and strive to help and uplift one another. Maybe you've noticed the same thing in your life.

> "Women are the key to a better world
> We need each other to create that world
> You and I are these women."

The international women I meet inspire me to do more and increase my awareness of how much needs to be achieved in the world. It's not a question of culture or location, every community in the world can benefit from more women leaders.

The world needs us to show up and unapologetically share our voices, visions, and values as authentic feminine leaders.

Chapter 11

Clarity in the Tropics

In 2015 after I blurted out my vision to a sea of women at the World YWCA World Council in Thailand, and well before IWL existed, I needed the steps to make it a reality. Nevertheless, as often happens following a conference or an inspiring speech, I stepped back into life as usual. Although I admit, in my case, nothing is ordinary about my life, and I like it that way.

My vision is a world of peace, understanding, and collaboration where each individual is valued and respected for her or his uniqueness. Lofty, right?

First, I needed to clarify how I would get there, regardless of where the universe was taking me.

Days later, I found myself sitting in my cozy corner at home on a comfortable couch in what I call my creative space. As I was sitting there with a steaming cup of coffee, that niggling thought came to me, "Okay, Bonnie, if that is your vision, what will you do about it?"

I wasn't always great with focus and organization. My husband Gérard was my key support system throughout our marriage. He believed in me even when I didn't think I was ready. When I shared my vision with him, he said, "Well then, make it happen."

Make it happen? How?

So, where to begin? In my experience, the universe responds when you have a question and throw it out there. In this case, the response was in the form of an invitation to attend a five-day Mastermind in Costa Rica the following March of 2016.

Lifelong learning is my passion, and the facilitator specialized in accountability. I believed the trip would help me implement my vision. To be honest, when I accepted, I had thought I would focus on growing my present organization, *AgeEsteem*. My idea was to use its success to finance acting on my new vision.

Costa Rica was magical, and the journey itself was captivating. The voyage took a few hours from the airport to the hotel. Riding in the minibus, we stopped to stand on a bridge overlooking crocodiles. Crocs the size of army tanks floated on the glistening river. Their sheer size dashed any previously held awe of the American alligators.

Our small group booked an entire coastal resort for the weeklong event.

The air was hot and humid yet had that earthy smell of foliage you inhaled with every breath. The unusual sounds of insects were mesmerizing, like an intricate jazz song to my ears; it filled my brain. The beetles were the size of the palm of my hand, like no insect I had ever seen, almost prehistoric.

Imagine those mornings when you awaken from a restful sleep, your body stretches, and your face has a smile arising from deep within you. There's nothing better unless, of course, you find yourself in Costa Rica and can roll out of bed right into a sparkling pool. Being surrounded by ocean and pool water was supportive, nurturing, and therapeutic.

Waking up that way, you know everything is possible.

The foods were equally alluring, bright, luscious, and nutritious, everything you'd expect with tropical tastes and abundant fresh seafood.

Although I wasn't consciously aware of it, change, transformation, clarity, focus, and plans were manifesting. I realize now that the mastermind's momentum commenced before the actual scheduled events of the week had started.

As our group totalled only five plus the facilitator, each attendee had two half days of concentrated time to focus on their project.

I already knew that I wanted to mentor, not coach women. I've probably coached 1,000 people in my life. But mentoring is different; I don't tell you what to do or help you set a goal or steps to reach that goal, nor will you discover your purpose at the end of the rainbow.

Instead, the mentee is the creator; her vision already exists. The concept is more significant than any goal. As a mentee, you go through profound self-discovery achieving confidence and clarity so you can authentically move closer to your vision.

I strengthen my connection with the universe when I stretch beyond my comfort zone and embrace life's adventures. Profound shifts at the heart and soul level occur when you're receptive to letting go and allowing the universe to lead.

I always keep an open mind. Once you have an expectation, you've shut down the flow of ideas and can overlook essential guidance and creative solutions. Similarly, if you narrow your focus, you limit your ability to see broader possibilities.

When it was my turn, the mastermind group asked deep and probing questions and challenged me to clarify, define and name what I needed. Within minutes of my first half day, I shared the mentoring program for women leaders and what would become Inspired Women Lead. I wanted more women at all levels and in all areas of leadership around the globe. The others quickly shared my excitement, and the idea began formulating with emotion and color.

I knew what I was building had to be sustainable without me. Too often, organizations become tied to one person, and when that person moves on, the association folds. This creation had to be about something greater! It also needed to have a global reach. The women had to live around the world, immersed in diverse cultures.

The hotel owners also owned a small island off the coast that we overlooked from our property. One of our final mastermind events took place on this enchanting island.

A tiny boat and captain ferried three of us at a time to the island. From the drop-off point, we walked across the island to be amongst the trees. I heard the sounds of water lapping onto the shore. Hammocks and a small kitchen awaited our arrival with another delicious meal of fresh fish from the sea.

We watched as more magic happened. The sun set lower in the sky, moving through the hues of pinks, corals, and oranges, and kissing the blue and green of the ocean. In an instant, the moon appeared full and brilliant in the sky.

We glided into the water and let our bodies float while watching the moon and stars. It might not seem like much, yet for me, it was powerful, and my new vision became even more vivid. The week had gone by too quickly, though so much was unearthed.

The mastermind helped crystallize what I needed next and how to bring my vision to life. While I'm spontaneous and live in the moment, I also take time to process, reflect, and find perspective. That week, I met another participant who was a coach and who understood my vision. As we were leaving our beautiful bubble, I acted quickly and hired her.

I've had many coaches throughout my life. Being able to bounce ideas and get professional guidance is helpful, especially when stepping outside of what you are emotionally attached to and gaining a new perspective.

My coach understood that transforming lives and positively changing the world were more important than the money aspect to me. I wanted the mentoring to be accessible to all women across the globe. A fee would have eliminated many women from the program, and that wasn't acceptable.

The most helpful message I received from my coach was that I couldn't wait for everything to be perfect because I would never be ready. There would always be a reason to put off starting. I had to act and adjust as things developed. I realized it was okay to be refining the application process while the first group of women was in the midst of their first cycle.

Once back home in Switzerland, things fell into place. The Costa Rica trip was in March 2016, and by June 2016, Inspired Women Lead became a reality! The mastermind helped me progress from stating the vision to launching the program.

If you have a dream or a whisper of a vision in your mind, don't worry if you don't know what to do next. It will come to you. Ask any of the women in IWL, and they'll tell you that if you're open and willing to keep going after your vision, nothing can stop you.

Without belief, a vision has little chance of manifesting.

Remember: One woman can change the world!

Why not YOU?

Attracting My Tribe

It is the power of a vision to draw the right people to us. I have been blessed by attracting many.

As the first mentees were finishing their mentoring cycle, we were gearing up for the third intake of mentees. To my delight, IWL was fully operational! However, its predicted growth would require a team. From its inception, I envisioned IWL as being led by several women with an equal voice in decisions.

In 2017, Andrea Oostenrijk, one of the very first mentees, designed our first logo, banner, and business card, which portrayed our vision and mission beautifully in color and design.

When I was speaking in Houston, Texas, a man came up to me, put his card in my hand, and said, "Your website is taken care of." Paul Taubman of Digital Maestro offered to create our original website and introduced us to other organizations.

Almost simultaneously with my thoughts, Annette Ebbinghaus, who would complete her mentoring in June 2017, said, "Bonnie, IWL is becoming too successful for one person to manage; I'd like to help. Why don't we plan a strategy session to see how to carry it forward?" Having been her mentor, I was confident we could create something special together.

This offer resulted in IWL's first strategy session, held in our living room in July 2017 with Annette Ebbinghaus, Margherita Brodbeck Roth, both Alumnae of IWL, and me. To complement us, we chose three women from the outside to broaden our perspective. These women had not heard of the IWL program - Dr Heather Cairns Lee (Education), Nora Cantini (NGO), and Catherine Birchara (Corporate). Heather, who teaches at IMD (International Institute for Management Development) Business School, generously offered to facilitate our session.

Our task was:
1. To define a business model to make Inspired Women Lead (IWL) financially sustainable, keeping these two conditions:
    a. The mentoring is FREE, which equalizes the opportunity.
    b. Finances do not depend on constantly seeking sponsors or grants. Instead, the source is to be ongoing residual income from partnerships with organizations who believe

in the mission of IWL. Until this time, the limited expenses of the program had been supported by my husband Gérard and myself.
2. Decide the best legal entity for Inspired Women Lead (IWL) based on our business model.

Situation as of 2017

Inspired Women Lead (IWL) was growing exponentially, doubling every six months.

> June 2016: 10 mentees (7 completed, 3 who dropped out, 2 of whom returned to the next session)
>
> June 2017: 51 mentors & mentees (4 mentoring for the second time)(Based on reasonable statistics, we were already impacting over 500,000 lives!)
>
> December 2017: the number of mentors and mentees impacted well over one million lives.

The session's outcome was to create a Swiss Association, which by definition, is owned by its members rather than any individual. Accordingly, the Charter Members became Bonnie Fatio, Annette Ebbinghaus, Margherita Brodbeck Roth, and Laetitia Fatio Gaillard as Swiss residents, with Geraldine Ang of Singapore and Andrea Oostenrijk of the USA.

All, except Laetitia, they formed the first Executive Council. Each council member carries an equal voice.

Shortly following, a Marketing Task Force, led by Geraldine Ang with branding specialist Shelley Hofer, formed to define our IWL brand. The team finalized the wording of our vision, mission, and values and defined our diverse audiences and donors and our common voice.

Chapter 12

The Love and Support of a Strong Man

My husband, Gérard, was an essential part of Inspired Women Lead, and I genuinely believe it would not exist if I had not had his continuous support. He encouraged me to stretch myself in ways that led me to grow. Although I had doubts, he never questioned whether I could do anything; he knew I could achieve whatever I set out to do, which made all the difference.

I met my future husband when I was 19; we married just after I turned 22. Ours was not a whirlwind romance, yet we both realized from the beginning that there was something extraordinary in the other, and though he would be in the States for only a year, there was no rush. Instead, we could take our time getting to know each other and sharing our dreams for the future.

At the time, I was a student at Michigan State University, teaching in Saint Joseph, MI, as part of my studies. He was working with Whirlpool to learn the American way of doing business. He was Swiss, from an old Geneva family, and spoke limited English with a delightful French accent.

With Gérard's broken English and my American English, I knew we would have to make allowances for misunderstandings when we spoke. Truly giving others the benefit of the doubt is a great gift to carry through life.

On our first walk on the beach on Lake Michigan, he fought off a dragon, took me on an imaginary cable car ride, and picked me a bouquet of reeds. Next, on the opening night of a play I was in, he presented me with a single rose. Then on a subsequent walk on the beach, on a balmy spring evening with romance in the air, I felt whatever this young man said would fill my heart. Gérard turned to me and said, "You're a witch."

Stunned for a moment, I, fortunately, found the presence of mind to ask him what he meant. "You're a fairy," he said. Then following a moment of reflection, I asked if he could explain what he meant. "Well, you're like Tinkerbell, always doing nice things for others." It's good to ask for clarification, right?

I mention those three memories because they set him apart from anyone else I had dated. Unlike other suitors, he did not shower me with gifts; instead, he showered me with special attention based on his imagination and playfulness. Huge bouquets are beautiful, although they can't compare to the true beauty I saw in that stunning single rose.

Following our wedding, we moved to Switzerland from the United States, where I had lived my entire life. So I arrived in a country where I didn't speak the language, in a new culture with multiple idiosyncrasies, and with a new family who was very present.

It was a huge adjustment, yet Gérard encouraged me by saying he admired how I was adopting and adapting to this new life. Never once did he criticize me for my lack of proper French, my points of view, or my highly spontaneous silly side, which brought an odd flavor to the more reserved Swiss culture.

However, as I tried to be the "Mrs Fatio" I thought Swiss culture expected, I was playing a role. I wasn't being me. Finally, after about 18 months, I returned to the States for a visit, during which I realized all I had to do to be accepted was just to be me. How often have we, as women, tried to fit in when all we need to be is our authentic selves?

> "It takes a man who knows who he is and is secure in himself to be able to fully support a woman."
>
> Baraz Samiian

As I made my way in my new country, I became sought after to help multiple organizations. There was even a period when Gérard laughed about being the 'prince consort'.

Due to one of my leadership positions, on several occasions, he was introduced as "the husband of" Bonnie Fatio. In a culture that is still patriarchal, it was a sign of a very secure man who could handle being second, even for an evening. Of course, Gérard had his own identity in the business world, community, and in sports as a skier and a sailor. He was well-known and admired for his integrity.

During my involvement with the World YWCA, we would receive the international board members at our home while they were in Geneva for a week of meetings. A highlight of those evenings would be Gérard's speech in which he applauded the women on the importance of their contributions to their organization and the world. He gave a similar speech at the IWL Champagne Reception of the 2019 World Event.

He was always proud of me, and we often joked about both specializing in renewable energies; he dealt with the technology side, and I with the human side.

Through the years, his friends have told me that I was the best thing to have happened to him. I know for sure that I am better for having had him in my life.

We complemented each other in almost every way. He was a thinker and a builder who loved to finalize a project. While he was thinking it through, I would finish a project or two with my usual spontaneity and often action came before complete thought. Over time we learned from each other. He taught me how to slow down and think, which helped me successfully create my businesses.

Gérard was one of the most balanced people I know, and I use the word balance purposely. He did not worry about situations where you could do nothing, instead, Gérard sought solutions. For example, I remember an evening when Gérard illegally parked our car. Just after he'd gotten into bed, I heard a racket outside and looked out of the window just in time to see our car being towed away. When I told him what was happening, he said, "There's nothing we can do about it tonight, so we might just as well go to sleep."

All this is to say that the love, understanding, encouragement, and emotional support that he managed to give me throughout the 55 years is a vital factor in what I have been able to accomplish, building to what I do today.

Observing our relationship, women often have asked me what advice I would offer for a happy marriage. Of course, my first thought is to marry somebody with comparable values who has integrity. Then I think about my grandmother.

While at university, I was dating a basketball star. When my grandparents asked me about him, I offered to bring him with me the next time I visited. Grandma's response is one I share often. She said, "If this is the man you will respect, trust, and be proud to introduce as the father of your children, then we would like to meet him." Gérard was the only one I ever took to meet them.

He kept family a priority even in the most stressful times. For example, on the day our daughter turned 18, he took her to the jeweler to offer her something she treasured. He kept his attention on her and made her day special while seamlessly juggling vital work negotiations.

Most importantly, he never held me back or made me feel I should stay at home because I was a woman. The first time I was asked to travel for my job, it fell during school vacation. When I mentioned it at the dinner table, Gérard's reaction was, "I'll take vacation then." It was wonderful. He never made me choose or feel guilty because he recognized the importance of my work and the importance of him being a good partner and father.

Now I could take my business trip without feeling remorseful, and my husband and daughter ended up taking the night train to Venice and had a marvelous time as a twosome. There were times following that trip when something would happen, and the two of them would look at each other and burst into laughter, all because of shared memories. Feeling the bond they created always warmed my heart.

 I've always been free to meet with friends, be they male or female, without any apprehension over how my husband will react. We both felt it was essential to have separate and mutual friends. This freedom opened opportunities outside of work for my participation in organizations like the World YWCA, High

Commission for Refugees, United Nations task force for equal opportunities for women, and many more.

What I'm trying to share here is the importance of mutual respect, trust, and pride, which allowed us to develop individually as well as a couple. It also meant recognizing the qualities in each other and the potential while helping that potential develop, even if that meant travel or absences.

Gérard was my constant model of integrity and authenticity. He was interested, curious, caring, and generous. Such as, when the company he directed laid off many employees, he chose to be present, to let each individual know they mattered, and to assist them in finding their next job.

I miss having his constant approval and encouragement. Still, Gérard remains within me as a perpetual standard for what I do.

Chapter 13

From Culture Shock To Catalyst for Gender Equality

In the fall of 2016, I was in Rome, Italy, to receive the WIN Global Inspiring Women Worldwide award. Since IWL and WIN's philosophies are closely aligned, I was honored to receive this prestigious award.

Upon arriving, the room was full of excitement. As I paused to figure out where I needed to be, another woman glowing with anticipation offered to assist me, and she's been in my life ever since.

Back then, Andrea Delannoy was a reserved yet charismatic woman. Today, she's a true authentic feminine leader. Her association MOD-ELLE is on a mission to broaden the Swiss perception of gender roles in the workplace through educating school-aged children.

Witnessing her IWL journey was like watching magic. It felt as if someone said "abracadabra," and suddenly, the empowered Andrea stepped forward.

Here's Andrea's story:

> Andrea Delannoy, originally from Romania, had worked for the Romanian Court of Audit. However, once she moved to Switzerland, she struggled to break into the field, so she retrained.
>
> She became a business manager for a consulting company assisting expat women in integrating professionally into Switzerland. In this new role, she built networks of people and discovered it was a natural fit for her "connecting the dots" mind.
>
> Having two daughters, she found the Swiss approach toward gender roles biased and limiting. She wanted her two daughters to grow up knowing they had endless career options.
>
> Andrea says, "it was a culture shock for me since Romanian policies foster gender equality in education and employment."
>
> In particular, she felt that, like most countries, Switzerland could be more proactive in attracting women to Math, Information Technology, Science, and Technology (MINT) careers. So, in 2011 she co-founded the charity Association Elargis Tes Horizons in Geneva

to promote science and science careers for girls.

Andrea thought, "What else can I do to support my daughters and other young women pursuing professional careers?"

Fortunately, when she was looking to further her leadership skills, gain clarity, and boost her confidence, she met Bonnie Fatio.

As a WIN member, Andrea attended their fall 2016 conference in Rome. There, Bonnie received WIN's highest award. Feeling their meeting was destined, she went straight up to Bonnie after the presentation and asked, "Will you be my mentor?"

Bonnie told her about Inspired Women Lead, and without hesitation, Andrea applied for and was accepted into the 2017 session. Being a self-described Cartesian, loving logical analysis, Andrea sincerely appreciated the program's structure.

She says, "it was a luxury to have Bonnie as my direct mentor. Her wisdom is genius."

"Although I had been very confident in Romania, I found life in Switzerland confusing for women," she says. Yet, something shifted when Bonnie became her mentor. "Bonnie helped me get back my inner strength. I found the courage to express my vision and felt certain I would achieve it," says Andrea.

Her vision is straightforward and profound: "to be a catalyst of change helping Switzerland progress on gender equality."

When Andrea became a mentor with access to the IWL Mentoring Guide, she realized that it was the key to IWL's success in replicating its process, results, and consistency.

After completing the IWL program, she found a UK charity conducting an in-depth international survey focusing on what influences children's career aspirations. She was invited to collect the Swiss data. The survey topic was no mere coincidence; it directly related to her newly stated vision.

The results demonstrated that gender stereotypes largely influence children's aspirations globally. It further identified that these attitudes begin to crystallize around age five. The findings were the a-ha moment for her that triggered the creation of MOD-ELLE.

She presented to the local education department a pilot program working with primary school children to tackle gender stereotypes in career aspirations.

As of 2022, MOD-ELLE offers three age-appropriate workshops, and over 170 women role models from all walks of life participate in the program. They visit primary schools and teach girls and boys, ages four to twelve, about the countless career possibilities available. So far, more than 1,600 children have completed the curriculum.

While the changes are slow, Andrea celebrates the shifting perceptions and says, "There is still much work to be done by schools, government, and local enterprises."

Here's an example of how children overcome gender bias in her school workshops.

One day a female police officer with the K-9 drug unit was assigned to visit a class as a role model. Visitors arrive wearing nondescript clothing, and the kids try to guess their occupations.

When the officer returned to the classroom in her uniform with her dog, one boy severely afraid of dogs was allowed to leave the room. He stood in the hallway, watching through the window, then cracked the door open for a better view.

The boy watched as his excited classmates asked questions and interacted with the officer and dog. Next, his teacher noticed his feet cross the door's threshold, and suddenly he was in the class and petting the dog just like his classmates.

After the presentation, the teacher asked the class about their thoughts on a woman as a law officer. This little boy proudly stood up and said: "I want to be a female police officer." The awareness training is as impactful for boys as it is for girls.

The in-class workshop challenges the children's perceptions while demonstrating that women can do and be anything.

MOD-ELLE's school program is expanding into additional Swiss regions, and Andrea is engaged in fundraising to ensure MOD-ELLE's longevity.

Additionally, she's designed a digital platform for teachers and volunteers to use the program regularly. This automation allows teachers to select and schedule their volunteer role models online from a current and wide-ranging list of female professionals.

Her daughters are pursuing non-traditional careers for Swiss women, which makes Andrea proud. Her eldest will study medicine, and the younger plans to study law.

The most significant takeaway from her time with IWL involved finding more life balance. She says, "I went from very little personal focus to a dramatically expanded one that reflects my new rich personal life."

Every woman will find IWL an asset in her life. You'll be challenged and supported throughout the year as you stretch, define, and refine how you see yourself. So, make a plan for the commitment and go for it.

She says, "My work doesn't feel like work, and I have more balance."

Chapter 14

Intergenerational Guidance

Loving Laetitia

When my daughter left home for the first time, I pondered what knowledge I could share with her and what I most wanted her to understand. I thought about which stories I could share and what insights would benefit her both then and later as she developed into a woman and eventually a mother.

The contemplation was interesting. I reflected on lessons from my life that could explain to her a parent's impact on their children. I wanted her to know I had tried to support her in a way that allowed her room to grow and discover the world on her terms rather than through my "advice" or guidance.

I come from intelligent, strong women who showed me how to realize a fulfilled life. My mother was a writer, published in magazines, and wrote seven books, despite the loss of her sight. She also broke the mold and convinced my father that a minister's wife could work outside the home. She eventually worked as a teacher. Women in the 1950s didn't buck the system, yet, her determination to follow her vision overrode any sense of doubt she might have felt.

I also learned a great deal from my maternal grandmother, who once told me, "The heritage we give to our offspring is not about money; it's much richer. It's about values and helping humanity by doing the right thing for the right reasons."

These two women had a profound effect on my development and my self-image. As a champion of women, I felt it was essential to give my daughter the same, if not more, wisdom than I received. Like Andrea Delannoy, who dreamed for her daughters, I wanted my daughter to tap into her full potential and know that she could be anything she envisioned, that all opportunities were available.

One of my earliest memories is a story about leadership, parenting, supporting children to realize their aspirations, and much more. What's truly remarkable was that I was not quite five years old when the lesson occurred. Since then, I have often thought about how significant that sequence of events was to my personal development.

I chose this story to share with my daughter, hoping it would impart meaning far beyond the words on the page.

> **❝** Some of my most influential role models are people who have transited my life in a matter of hours or minutes, yet their impact remains and permeates many of my actions. **❞**
>
> Bonnie Fatio

Here is an excerpt of my letter to my daughter:

> It was in Parchment, Michigan, that I had my first experience in stretching boundaries. I was not yet in school, so not quite five. I will never know what spurred me, but I asked Mom if I could take a walk with Danny. Now "a walk" to Mom at that time would mean to go around the block, which was a big block for a child. Of course, even at five, I knew this. Danny lived across the street, but he was at our house to play. So off we went. I proceeded to stop at the home of every friend that we had on our block and then crossed to Danny's side to gather more of our friends there. It was like a parade! I remember more than one mother asking if I had permission to be on their side of the street, meaning, "Does

Bonnie, aged 6, and her first boyfriend

your mom know what you are doing?" At least, that was how I interpreted it. She had said I could take a walk, so I replied that "Yes, my mom had said I could."

Well, as our little group grew, it seemed natural to focus on a destination. So off we marched to the park where we would pretend to be on a picnic. This meant crossing yet a second street, but one that we all knew well. What a wonderful time we had! We were all playing on the swings and in the sandbox when suddenly several cars arrived, and mothers were soon swarming all over the place! A lasting image is that of each child being solidly spanked by their mother, except for me.

Obviously, I did know that I was the bad one. I was the one who had stretched the truth and crossed not one but two streets. When I asked Mom why she did not spank me, I remember she said something about "Spanking will not change what you did. Wait until your father gets home!"

Neither of our parents had ever spanked us, but this sounded threatening. When Daddy arrived home that afternoon, I was cowering behind the tall drapes in the living room. Oh, he knew that I was there, but I nevertheless felt invisible as I waited to see what his wrath might be.

After Mom had given him a full synopsis of what had transpired and my role as instigator, he turned to her and snorted as he sometimes did when something caught his sense of humor and said, "Shirley, I told you Bonnie would be a natural leader!" And that was all we ever heard about it, except for me inquiring of Mom what a leader was. And what a relief to learn that it was neither criminal nor disease.

Would Daddy have remembered this incident? Probably not. However, that lesson has remained in my memory all of these years as an important one. There is more to leading than being at the front of a parade of followers. We have to consider the ethics and outcome of what we do. What a lesson it was in thinking about your own acts and the influence that they can have on others. The innocents were spanked. Though trembling in my hiding place when Daddy came home, I actually received commendation rather than condemnation. Had I been spanked, would my life be different today?

These seemingly insignificant events do, I believe, mold our lives in greater ways than we can imagine. They stand alone, then build on the previous and become a foundation for what follows. If you only knew, sweet Laetitia, how often I have tried to choose my words and actions in order to give you what I hoped to be the right signals and examples, the appropriate encouragement and direction. Even more, how often I have kept quiet in order to free you to make your own choices and experiences.

Our Little Kon-Tiki

Beyond family, you never know who will shape you. Life-changing moments can happen anywhere, anytime. For me, the most memorable are those people who, with their quiet wisdom, fostered a deeper level of self-discovery. They include an unexpected encounter with a forest ranger and a life-long mentorship with a spiritual advisor.

My parents, two younger sisters, and I loved camping; my older sister preferred to stay home with a summer job. So, one summer, we packed the car and drove cross-country from our home in Pennsylvania to Yosemite National Park in California.

Precise organization is key to any great camping trip, especially for a family of five. Our large tent accommodated our entire family, and we became experts at setting it up and taking it down. We must have pitched that tent 29 times during our travels that summer. We all had jobs to set up and take down our campsites. In 45 minutes, we were either camping or ready to hit the road.

The Yosemite trip was a trip of a lifetime. It's one of the most spectacular national parks in the United States. The events that unfolded were transformational.

Attending an open-air church service surrounded by majestic trees and rugged mountains was a communication with nature and God. After one service, unfortunately, my father leaped to his feet and became ill. It was several frightening minutes as time dragged on.

His symptoms indicated a heart attack. Fortunately, we soon discovered it was altitude sickness. A young man attending the service, with little girls climbing all over him, had stepped in to help. His name was Haakon David Carlson, and he was a PhD student from Minnesota. The little girls had adopted him as apparently many children did; he was considered the Pied Piper of Yosemite. He worked every summer as a forest ranger at the park. Haakon asked to show me around the park.

With my parents' permission, off I went on an adventure. It was one of those balmy summer days when it felt good to be in the shade of a tree or a cool stream. A day where you stretch your arms out and lift your head to the sky, smiling and laughing because it feels good to be alive.

On our hike, we came upon the remnants of a raft-like structure that had seen better days. In fact, our little Kon-tiki wasn't water-worthy when we stumbled upon it.

We gathered what we could find and made enough repairs that we were able to ride her down the river. Our excitement was palpable. We took something that appeared useless and made it functional once more.

At some point, we left the raft on the shore for another lucky person to find. The day was already so much more than I could've expected.

Haakon began asking me about my dreams and ambitions as we rested in the shade. What did I want for my life? This forest ranger was some ten years my senior yet showed a genuine interest in me, a 16-year-old, and my life's goals.

Although I was deeply affected by Dr King's speech only weeks before, I hadn't yet thought about future dreams, my mission, or a vision for my life. Haakon was the first person to ask and said he saw a quality in me. Something special.

He made me believe it too. Until then, people looked at me as a tall, pretty blonde girl with long legs. Young men treated me as nothing more than another pretty face. They never spoke to me as an individual with a brain or gift to offer the world.

Being treated as an intellectual was a new experience and opened my mind to new possibilities. It was overwhelming.

I felt the Creator was opening his arms for me, enveloping me in his embrace. The depth of understanding, warmth, and love I felt was significant. Somehow, as we sat and talked, we had become part of the majestic sequoias surrounding us.

Since then, only Gérard has ever asked me such meaningful and intense questions. I would not be the woman I am today without the encouragement I received all those years ago. Thank you, Haakon David Carlson, PhD student, and forest ranger.

You never know who will cross your path or how your course will alter. That day my path broadened, and I found an inner knowing that "yes," I have a gift for the world.

My Spiritual Mentor

Delbert (Deb) Jolley was a pastor in one of the churches in the same Pennsylvania conference as my dad and was responsible for the regional youth program. I became active in this program at age 12, and as I took on leadership positions at the regional level during my teen years, Deb became a strong influence in my life.

We all tried to attend the camp week that he led each summer. I was a bit strong-minded, surprise, surprise, and thinking no one would miss me one day, I decided to hike down the mountain to get myself an ice cream at the little grocery store. That night at dinner, Deb strolled over to our table and casually asked, "Was the walk worth it?" He never reprimanded me for anything, and there were occasions when he could have. Instead, he simply let me know that he accepted me as I was and who I was becoming.

I told Deb in my teens that I wanted him to officiate at my wedding. So, despite having a minister father and grandfather who would participate in the service, Deb also officiated. Gérard and I often joked that it took three pastors to tie our wedding knot, which made it more solid than any other.

I refer to Deb as my Spiritual Mentor, who remained so until he died at age 96. In fact, when my husband asked me what I wanted to do for our 25th wedding anniversary, I responded, "spend it with Deb." So, we flew over the Atlantic, drove to the assisted living home in Pennsylvania, where he lived, and spent 48 hours with him and his wife. That's how important he was.

People like Deb and my parents, who accompanied me on all or significant parts of my life journey, and so many others, have instilled in me the richness of love, friendship, encouragement, and having a guiding light. Such relationships are life's greatest gift, and I am eternally grateful for them.

One person ignites something within another person, and the world transforms.

Can it be that simple? ***Yes!***

The mission for Inspired Women Lead (IWL) works just this way. We help one woman at a time transform. Self-discovery uncovers the spark that stokes her fire. At the same time, she develops the tools to make a difference, acting on her vision.

Seeing My Vision Through Their Eyes

> " Every time I work with women who live in different cultures and countries, I feel inspired by my own leadership. We each constantly learn and grow in our leadership when we open our hearts and minds to each other. "
>
> Bonnie Fatio

Sometimes you wonder if what you're creating will be as significant as you envision. The first IWL World Event gathering proved to me that we were on the right track. I witnessed my vision living through these women.

Once we established the organization's internal structure, we planned our first-ever world event. Held in Geneva, Switzerland, in the Summer of 2019, this was the next major milestone for Inspired Women Lead, with 42 women arriving from multiple countries.

All of the women had built strong relationships even though, until this point, they had only met virtually. For these women to suddenly see each other in person was incredible! Imagine the immense joy upon finally seeing the woman you spent all that time getting to know and witnessing her journey. There were moments when the surprise was voiced with an overwhelming, "Oh my goodness, there's my mentor!"

The first evening was one of these beautiful summer evenings that refused to let you stay indoors. We had chosen our venue for its huge esplanade so the welcome reception could be outside. The view of Mont Blanc was breathtaking. Seeing everyone who had grown so close through the program was beautiful.

Elsa Ferreira, from the first mentee group, was the organizer and point person for the event. When she told me it was time for my welcome address, I said, "Look around. I'm not going to interrupt this ambiance; everyone is already connecting and feeling welcome."

Impressed by the positive energy and excitement, the hotel staff got caught up in the buzz from our party. Beyond a buzz, it felt like fireworks or electric energy that multiplied like swimming in a sea of fireflies.

I saw the power of the mentoring journey and the bond it created. It exceeded my wildest dreams!

The following two days, we had IWL women conduct workshops based on the program's themes. Each had its own flavor and was empowering. One of these was a brainstorming session to explore what women wanted for the future of IWL. Their wish list would become the basis of discussion at the strategy meeting of the Executive Council in the fall.

We were privileged to have Skyguide and Air France as sponsors during the event, which allowed us to bring in our guest speaker and offer scholarships for women who would otherwise be unable to attend.

Other highlights of the World Event were:
- IWL scarf, created by Anouke Kluiters
- IWL music logo created by Catarina Reis and her husband
- Special guest speakers open to the public
- Champagne Cocktail in a private garden in Old Town Geneva
- Celebration Dinner

The most excellent highlight was simply being together in person!

Following the success of the summer event, the Executive Council met for a strategy session in London in October 2019. Among the items on the agenda was reviewing the wish list from the world event. All suggestions were considered as we set the strategy for the coming years. It was most important to set up a partnership task force to develop revenue sources to sustain the association.

One of our decisions was to review and revise the Mentoring Guide. Although I had updated it regularly, it seemed an excellent idea to bring together a task force of women from different regions of the world to review and revise it.

So, in March 2020, I brought together six teams of three women representing different regions. They did a fantastic job, and the results are reflected in the guide as it is today. Now a team of two, Mafalda Pereira and Claudia Gras from Portugal and Italy, respectively, consider ongoing suggestions for both the guide and its annexes.

Chapter 15

Promise to Save Daughters Saves Thousands

I well remember meeting Josephine Ndirias at the highly attended 2019 Female Wave of Change (FWoC) Global Conference in South Africa.

She was relatively reserved yet shone, revealing something extraordinary within, something that still begged to be set free. I wanted to tap into the gifts she had to offer the world. The day we met, she wore her beautiful Maasai dress with pride and presence; she was very charismatic.

FWoC, founded by Ingun Bol in 2017, is doing meaningful work worldwide. Their goals align with many of my values and vision to empower women and nurture authentic feminine leaders. They educate women in more than 40 countries to bring awareness that women are the key to improving the world we leave for future generations.

The 2019 conference theme was Creating the Future We Want. As an FWoC Global Ambassador, I spoke on Achieving Tangible Results Together

A complete surprise for me during the event was to receive the ***Female Wave of Change "Accelerating the Change Process and Re-Creating the Future" award.*** (Jacinda Ardern, former Prime Minister of New Zealand, was also awarded at this ceremony.)

Ingun Bol (FWoC Founder), Dr Khomotso Malete and Bonnie Fatio

I never tire of seeing the many joyful faces at these events, women ready to make a change in their own lives and for women worldwide. The mutual desire to create a world where all women are empowered and treated with respect creates momentum for all participants.

Josephine's story profoundly impacted me. Like many mothers, her vision began with keeping her daughters safe.

Here's Josephine's story:

> Before meeting Bonnie Fatio, Josephine Ndirias was already on a mission to help her people, the Maasai, by taking on the serious cultural issues of forced child marriage and female genital mutilation(FGM). She ran a community-based organization in rural northern Kenya.
>
> As a mother of four daughters, she refused to let them be a statistic. Alternatively, she would find a way for her daughters and all girls of Kenya to no longer be married off at age 14 or have their genitals cut.
>
> For generations, FGM was a rite of passage; without it, the people believed that the girl was cursed. Large community celebrations ensued once the procedure concluded.
>
> While working with another organization, Josephine spent a year educating community leaders about the maltreatment, injury, and adverse effects of child marriage and FGM.

Unfortunately, the harm they were causing to girls wasn't enough for the men to stop the practice. Instead, she had to show the leaders that the financial burden was too heavy for the men and how the community suffered.

By the end of the year, her efforts and determination paid off. The community elders, the custodians of the Maasai culture, embraced a new tradition for the rite of passage called "Breaking the Curse." Their decision has already rescued more than 160 girls, thereby replacing the ancient custom.

Although it is now illegal in Kenya to perform FGM, the law alone hasn't completely eradicated the practice in the more rural areas.

In addition, Josephine's organization, Mukogodo Girls Empowerment Programme, provides education camps for the 14 and 15-year-old girls eligible for this transition. During the week, girls receive counseling on dating, life skills, and reproductive health, including plenty of dialogue opportunities. On the final day, the cultural elders come and conduct a big ceremony and bless their transition from girls to women.

This new mainstream event celebrates breaking the curse rather than harming the girls, honoring the culture more positively and beneficially for all.

Still looking to further her ability to affect even more change, Josephine attended a Female Wave of Change event in 2019. There, she heard Bonnie Fatio speak and knew she was in the right place at the right time as if fate had intervened.

So much of what Bonnie talked about that day moved her. She felt Inspired Women Lead (IWL) could help her reach more people, so Josephine knew she had to join IWL.

Josephine says, "IWL is an opportunity for women to connect and make our dream come true. We need each other to realize our potential. In simple terms, women's empowerment, in general, is the way to go. In my experience, women make good decisions for their children and family."

During the first six months, Josephine discovered herself and how best to put all her potential into practice. She became aware that self-love is not selfish. She also learned to set boundaries by saying "No" to the things she cannot do and "Yes" to those she can.

"The IWL program allows you to express yourself from your personal experiences and connects you deeply with the other person," says Josephine.

As the mentor, her mentee was European, the kind of go-getter who could wake up, have an idea, and jump in blindly at full speed. This concept was entirely unfamiliar to Josephine. She says, "After meeting my mentee, I learned to take more risks in my life. So even though I was her mentor, I learned much from her too."

Since the IWL program, Josephine has realized that everyone, not just women, needs mentoring. Consequently, she's adding a mentorship network to her empowerment program to create a ladder effect of support for each step of the growth cycle.

Individuals with more work experience mentor
→ those beginning to work who mentor
→ college students who mentor
→ secondary school children who mentor
→ primary school children

Josephine's organization and outside funding through charitable contributions have enabled more than 500 girls to obtain an education.

She has returned to university to study Social Dignity and Sociology, aimed at facilitating the dissemination of information on relevant topics in her community. She knows that education is vital to change, allowing more informed discussions, and ultimately transforming or ending retrogressive cultural practices in her country.

Isolated incidents of the illegal practice of FGM secretly continue in some rural communities. Roughly 40% of the Maasai people live in these areas. Josephine and other organizations continue their work to eliminate it.

Kenyan mothers and most women, in general, are wounded, and they don't know how to release or heal their pain. Subsequently, the pain passes from one generation to the next. "We help the mothers understand that their daughters can escape experiencing the same traumas and pains. If we want a generation of unwounded daughters, we must heal the mothers and help them raise their daughters with love," says Josephine.

Josephine evolved during her IWL experience, and her vision grew. She believes women will solve significant issues, including hunger, healthcare, financial independence, and decision-making at family and community levels.

She says, "If we want to change the world, we must empower women. Women are full of love and, when empowered, give back to society, family, and the next generation."

Chapter 16

Corporate Partners Find Success Formula with Inspired Women Lead

In 2023 we see companies challenged with the burden of balancing bottom-line profits with the demand for the production of goods and services and the development of their people.

Forward-thinkers at leading-edge companies acknowledge that people are the number one asset, the keystone of any business.

These companies go further than the rest taking leadership development to new levels by fostering a culture that promotes female development programs with an innovative approach. Programs like Inspired Women Lead (IWL) affect global change and create female leaders who lead as their authentic selves.

They stop expecting women to fit into the male role model and instead celebrate the qualities and traits that come naturally to women.

Inspired Women Lead is the right fit for any business that commits to developing its female staff. By becoming our partner, the women you choose to send through our mentoring program will be more confident in their leadership style. In addition, as described by some of our existing partner representatives and Alumnae, the results are tangible.

> **IWL isn't something more - IWL is something different.**
> Christiane Damal - Skyguide

A number of aspiring female associates from companies such as Hewlett Packard Enterprise®, Skyguide, Velocity Global®, Red Cross, and Unicef have completed the IWL program.

In Switzerland, there's now a government mandate that businesses reach a 20-30% ratio of women on boards and executive boards; make no mistake, this is a global issue. The mandate has forced businesses to step up because they weren't promoting women equally.

Businesses don't excel at leadership development for women. IWL prepares women and gives businesses a leadership program that's essentially a "plug and play." So, when women complete IWL, they're ready for that next step in their careers.

Skyguide is a Swiss-based air navigation service provider which manages and monitors Swiss airspace. Skyguide is under the umbrella of the Swiss government.

The aerospace industry and air traffic control are historically masculine environments. Traditionally, the more skilled and higher-paying positions of engineers and technicians are male-dominated.

In contrast, women primarily gravitate to human resources, finance, and marketing. Approximately 73% of Skyguide women are in non-management positions, and the higher the position, the fewer women, according to a Skyguide representative. However, in 2018 the company was aiming for women to hold 18% of the management slots, so they were keen on programs to achieve those means.

Because of the specialized air traffic jobs, employees tend to commit to long careers with Skyguide.

Catherine (Cate) Bichara of Skyguide was someone IWL brought in from the outside for our first strategy meeting in June 2017. She then joined the mentoring program in June 2018.

Seeing the benefits and value that IWL women offered companies, she spoke to colleague Christiane Damal, Head of People Development, Health Unit, and Diversity at Skyguide.

Skyguide's Diversity and Inclusion program was actively looking for something to help women promote themselves to the next level, improve confidence, take responsibility, and take the next step in their professional development. Other training programs were in place, yet Christiane felt the company needed something dedicated to women. So the time was perfect for

Skyguide to test out IWL's program.

When Christiane also realized that IWL is an international association, she felt the women would further benefit by developing deep relationships and a better understanding of other cultures, a much-needed skill set in our global world.

"As with all things Swiss, especially new ideas for companies, it takes more time to be implemented," Christiane says.

The first approach was determining how the program could roll out within Skyguide. Christiane invited me to speak to their women's group to share our work. At the end of the session, it was clear the women preferred not to have the program run in-house; instead, they wanted to join the existing program to have contact with women in other countries, cultures, and industries to gain new perspectives.

Christiane was excited that women could be themselves in this program. They wouldn't have to filter what they said or presented because no one from the company would be there watching how they came across. The mentees could fully engage in the program of self-discovery.

Initially, she identified three women from various departments who she deemed great candidates for management. Since she had the budget, Skyguide sponsored and paid for the three candidates.

In her and other managers' assessments, this unofficial first trial was a smashing success for the women and Skyguide.

The IWL Alumnae:
- Take more initiative
- Voice creative solutions for issues
- Identify how their skill set contributes
- Exhibit greater confidence
- Initiate collaborations with other areas

While her immediate boss was not supportive, Christiane did what many successful people do; she didn't take no for an answer. Instead, she went to CEO Alex Bristol, who gave her the go-ahead.

Skyguide officially began its partnership with IWL in 2017. Currently, the contract allows for three women annually; as of 2022, approximately 12 women have completed the program.

Christiane says, "At Skyguide, we feel professional development is the company's responsibility. We make the space for employees to acquire the skills necessary to be more valuable to the company, which makes for happy people. We trust our people, their work gets done, and we don't micromanage. Employees do this program on company time while feeling supported and without guilt."

Inspired Women Lead, with its unparalleled mentoring, addresses aspects that Skyguide or other official programs don't cover.

Satisfied with the results and seeing this new added value by the women, she believes that other companies get the same great results when their female employees participate in IWL.

Skyguide says about the IWL program, "We get very competent people with minimal time investment, and we're able to give them new responsibilities based on these new competencies."

Since 2017, our relationship has grown, and Skyguide helped sponsor our first World Event in July 2019 in Geneva, Switzerland.

IWL Alumnae Soar at Skyguide

Christiane shared a story about a recent IWL participant that she observed daily. Christiane had seen her high potential, though the woman didn't seem to know how to tap into it herself. She lacked the confidence to take initiative. Consequently, her manager often needed to give specific directions on tasks and projects and suggest collaborations within the office.

However, no one could deny the results of IWL. Managers commented, and Christiane observed how the employee took the initiative by volunteering her assistance and ideas. She sought collaborative opportunities where she could contribute and share her talents with others.

In addition, her demeanor shifted into a significantly more confident woman. Instead of quietly keeping to herself, she began asking "How can I bring something else to the company or a project; how can I help another person?"

She opened herself to her leadership abilities. She found her voice and actively sought ways in which her competencies would benefit the company. She told Christiane that her time in IWL was so amazing, letting her reflect on what she wanted privately.

It was the right program at the right time – when she needed it most.

The same is true for the other IWL Alumnae at Skyguide. They stand out because they know their worth and what they bring to the table. In addition, these women consciously find areas where their involvement benefits a colleague, project, and the company.

As a result of their female employees completing the IWL program, women have gained greater visibility and it has opened their candidatures for promotion, helping to increase the number of women in leadership positions.

Christiane told me the success formula is increasing competencies, getting participants out of their comfort zones, and taking over new responsibilities with more independence. Each woman has an enhanced ability to speak up. Their augmented communication skills are an asset.

The women selected for IWL come from various nationalities, such as Irish, German, Filipino, and Swiss. However, there is a universal theme that women worldwide have in common: ingrained traits or insecurities around speaking up and knowing their value because of societal and familial judgments.

IWL helps women find their voices regardless of where they come from or who they are – you go in as one person, and during the process, you uncover who you are and come out of the program a leader as your authentic feminine self.

At Skyguide, the IWL Alumnae realize that their competencies translate to many positions they would never have previously considered. So, now they apply for and are hired into management positions in non-traditional departments like engineering because of their strong leadership qualities.

Several women gave me their views on corporations wanting to partner with IWL. Here are their key points for Inspired Women Lead:

Structure:
The results have been replicated over and over. Despite the diversity of participants, the program is consistent cycle after cycle. The selection of mentor/mentee pairs and the environment created within the system are unprecedented. There is an "X" factor that can't be easily quantified. It just works. Women emerge as more vital team members and company leaders.

Diversity:
Connecting with others from around the world is a rich, eye-opening experience. The intercultural aspect and seeing life in real time through another woman is an experience you won't get anywhere else. The global dynamics make this facet timely, and women become global thinkers. All companies benefit, even companies not yet global benefit from this broader perspective.

Female Leadership:
Defining and understanding what it means and using that female part in leadership. Empathy, caring, and building relationships are integral parts of a business – without them, you miss out on the human aspect of human resources. Women naturally excel in these competencies if they're allowed to exhibit them.

In 2023 it's officially acceptable to have a mentor, and there are more choices of mentors than ever before. "IWL is set apart by its structure, diversity, and leadership results. The program design is genius," says Christiane.

Finding your voice is critical for any woman. Most will say they feel less effective and struggle more often without it. If you want to share an idea, stand up for yourself or someone else, get a promotion, or participate in meaningful ways, then at some point, your voice and opinions need to be clearly conveyed.

Chapter 17

Glossophobia - The Fear Of Public Speaking

Upwards of 75% of the world has some degree of fear of public speaking. For most, it ranks right up there with death, clowns, and poverty. No kidding!

The one class I actually skipped during high school was Public Speaking. I hated the idea of it, and like most of my student friends was filled with dread. Now I absolutely love sharing my message with diverse audiences.

My personal goal has always been to be a catalyst for positive change reaching as many people as possible. Therefore, I must be in front of people, connecting with them and delivering meaningful and inspirational messages leading them to take action.

Public speaking is a necessity for me, and I thrive on the energy exchanged between the listeners and myself.

I've had the honor of speaking around the world on every continent, except Antarctica. Throughout my life, public speaking engagements have found me. Word of mouth has been my most effective booking agent, whether in person, radio, or on television. I'll meet someone, or they'll hear me speak, then remember me and recommend me for a panel, show, or as a solo speaker.

In addition to various corporations, and regional and local conferences/meetings, a few of the prestigious venues where I have spoken are:

- World Health Organization (WHO) in Geneva, Switzerland
- International Labour Organization in Geneva, Switzerland
- YWCA World Council in Nairobi, Kenya
- Entrepreneurship Club, Harvard Business School, Cambridge, MA, USA
- WIN Conferences in Oslo, Norway; Paris, France; Rome, Italy
- The Leadership Training Institute in Bogota, Colombia
- Commission on the Status of Women, United Nations in New York, USA
- United Nations Retirement Program, United Nations in Geneva, Switzerland
- Dare to Dream Conference, Bournemouth, England
- Women's Leadership Forum, Bangkok, Thailand

- Young Women's Leadership Training, Katmandu, Nepal
- Female Wave of Change Conference in the Netherlands and their World Conference in Johannesburg, South Africa
- International University Women, Cape Town, South Africa

I've spoken about healthy aging, authentic women's leadership, personal growth, and how one person transforms the world. The specifics of a speech adjust to fit the overall theme of the event or venue.

My first experience speaking at the United Nations (UN) in Geneva was as part of a United Nations Symposium: Changing Business to Change the World: How can business become an active agent of development? October 2002. I was asked to speak on "The Broader Meaning of Service."

I admit that it was daunting the first time I spoke at the UN since Geneva is considered the capital of peace. In 1913 the UN was initially founded as the League of Nations. The building took my breath away; it's stately, impressive, and oozes history. I could almost hear the echoes of negotiations and decisions of a century past. Even as a tourist, I suspect you can feel the richness of history steeped in the walls.

Most of the rooms are large, and in the older section, they are dark. The hallways are labyrinth-like. Although you are security checked and given a pass when you enter, after that you are on your own. Heads of State are guarded and guided, whereas many times, I needed to ask for help to find my way.

As you can imagine, I prepared exceptionally well, knowing I had to be at my very finest. I presented with my flavor, which always includes audience participation. This style was not common practice: it caught the audience off guard. I was inviting them to participate plus offer creative ideas as to how they might better be of service as individuals, professionals, and organizations.

A long silence followed, and I called on all my strength to allow the silence to stretch until ideas finally began to break it.

Fortunately, it did turn out well in the end and resulted in invitations for me to speak at another conference. However, remembering it, I can still feel that silence in the pit of my stomach!

Since then, I've spoken several times in the context of different conferences at the United Nations, both in Geneva and in New York.

The United Nations in New York was being revamped and restored during two of the years that I spoke at the Commission on the Status of Women (CSW). Most of the non-plenary meetings are not in the actual UN building. However, when I spoke on a panel or led intergenerational dialogues within the hallowed walls of the UN, I always felt part of something much more powerful than myself or the mass of women present.

Similar to Geneva, so much world history occurred inside the UN in New York. It is an awe-inspiring and humbling experience to feel a part of that as you speak. Actress Reese Witherspoon had tears in her eyes as she expressed this same feeling during her speech to UN Women at the CSW.

Every opportunity creates a life lesson which is one of the

greatest gifts I receive. They make me think about what happened, give me perspective, and help me reassess and make course corrections. I improve with every opportunity.

I always want the audience to be enriched, more importantly, to think and ask what they can do next. Both speaker and audience walk away with more awareness.

My favorite pre-speech activity is mingling with the audience, hearing their stories, and discovering what's important to them. It's proven to be an advantage in multiple situations. When it's time for my speech, I'll share some of those stories to help the audience better connect to my points.

Not every speaking engagement goes as planned; sometimes, the organizers run into glitches and unforeseen delays. At one event, the torrential rain impacted guest arrival times, while simultaneously, we discovered that the ballroom was double booked.

The other half of the room was selling tickets to a world soccer match. As a result, the room was teeming with fans and the boisterous overzealous frenzy we associate with soccer crowds. In addition, the police shut down traffic which further impacted the evening.

Amid the raucous, I took advantage of the delays and did what I loved, I mingled. I met a 90-year-old woman eager to learn how to live her life more fully, a 50-year-old who had lost his job, and a couple who were now unexpectedly raising their grandchildren. Later, when I took the stage, I felt an intimate relationship with many people in the room.

Capitalizing on moments like these allows me to tailor my speeches using more pertinent examples that personally impact the listeners. By the time I get on stage or go on air, I feel that my audience is a small intimate group, and I'm speaking to friends.

Interacting with the group also allows me to settle into the group's rhythm. When I open my mouth, I forget everything except why I am there and connecting with people. I'm completely present in the moment.

One of my greatest lessons came from one of my first speaking engagements. I learned not to assume I know how an audience will or is responding to what I'm saying.

As I recall, there was no head table, so I sat among the crowd. We gathered at large round tables in fractured groups for dinner. The room was thick with negativity, and I felt disconnected. During my talk, I was nervous and bothered by the negative energy in the room.

The gentleman seated nearest to me kept rolling his eyes as I spoke. His attitude was just short of moaning his displeasure. Imagine my surprise when he was first in line to talk with me afterwards. Based on what I saw during the presentation, I was shocked by what he said.

First, he could almost recite my speech back to me; then, he told me how uplifted he felt by what I said. Next, he explained that he planned to use some of my techniques in his life. I could hardly believe what I had heard.

It was a genuine ah-ha moment, and I realized my assessment of the gentleman and our connection was entirely wrong.

That single encounter showed me not to be nervous or assume what the listeners feel. Since then, I have trusted that everything will work out.

It may amuse you that despite having spoken in prestigious places and to diverse audiences, one of my most intimidating experiences was being a keynote speaker at the Toastmasters Leadership Institute in Bern, Switzerland. Knowing that each person there was striving to be the best speaker possible made me wonder if they would evaluate my every word and gesture. However, they were receptive, and I thoroughly enjoyed the experience despite my apprehension.

Another strategy I employ in my presentations is observation and preparation. If there are other speakers scheduled before me or if I'm on a panel, I listen closely to what they're saying. I'll also research them ahead of the event. This conscious listening and research technique helps me more precisely use my speech to complement theirs. For example, I'll refer to something they've said and tie it to one of my points, helping the audience connect more deeply.

After any speech, depending on the setting, there is often a line of people with specific questions. Otherwise, I circulate among the crowd, answering questions, conversing, and listening to what they discover. Their ah-ha moments are the most gratifying to my soul.

It's essential to speak from my heart and show my optimistic personality. Considering the audience, I choose a natural look for my hair and makeup. That way, they always see my authentic self. I love color, so I often select bold blue, red, or pink. You won't find me showing up in a dark suit; I broke out of that "Male Box" long ago.

None of us should be labeled and put into a box. "Breaking out of the Male Box" is necessary for women to step up as authentic feminine leaders. Conversely, I'm not suggesting we create a female box to define women. The world is better when women and men are valued equally, complementing each other.

I'm fortunate to know so many diverse women who've found their voice and are changing the world. Through our discussions, I can gauge the relevance of my chosen topics, which add depth to my understanding and enrich my speeches.

Chapter 18

Authenticity Leads the Way to Personal Transformation

> " Authentic leadership removes the judgement and unburdens the mind. "
>
> Fides Nibasumba
> Burundi - Inspired Women Lead 2022

I am interested in people and yet am lousy with names. How it's possible not to remember meeting Sarah Fern is baffling. Yet when I met Sarah at a Women's Conference at the United Nations in Geneva in June 2022, I thought we were meeting in person for the first time. However, this time she left a lasting impression on me. She was engaging, articulate, and present in the moment, and you could feel the positive energy emanating from her.

Here's Sarah's Story:

Sometimes you don't even know what you are missing or that there could be another way until you catch a glimpse of a different reality.

Sarah Fern was a very successful, extremely busy human resource professional. Velocity Global®, where Sarah is the Chief People Officer, is America's fifth-largest company in recent private equity investments. So, it's a rocket ship, and she was basically working 24/7.

By all accounts, she was content with her present situation until an unexpected trip to Rome exposed her to another world of possibilities.

In 2018, amid a hectic schedule of six acquisitions in one year, Sarah agreed to step in and attend a conference in place of her boss. With little notice and even less time to prepare, she didn't know what to expect.

Until then, Sarah hadn't witnessed many positive role models for women in the business world. There seem to be two general stereotypes of women:

- the secretaries performing primarily clerical duties and appearing to play it a little bit dumb or a little sexy or
- the bossy women who dress like men because they need to be like the men to fit in for a chance to succeed

There wasn't anything in the middle, and neither seemed to be genuinely themselves.

Sarah says, "the WIN conference was the first time I had seen hundreds and hundreds of self-assured women come together like that. They were very global, confident, yet humble, and making an impact in the world." It was completely different from anything else she had ever witnessed.

One of the speakers, Bonnie Fatio, particularly impressed Sarah, and afterwards, Bonnie handed her a business card.

Returning home, Sarah was quickly absorbed back into the multiple acquisitions. Unfortunately, her demanding schedule didn't leave time to do anything with that business card. It quickly became buried under more current work.

Almost two years later, Sarah was immersed in a 2019 end-of-year cleanup in her home office and found Bonnie's card. She thought, "Okay, this year's going to be when I do something about it." She enrolled immediately!

As it happened, the next cohort started in June 2020, the world was in total COVID lockdown, and the program took on a new significance. Suddenly connecting with this global network of women who were so accessible became even more meaningful.

The IWL program was unique to Sarah because obtaining this level of training and networking usually costs a lot of money, and you're required to attend in person. Instead, IWL mentoring is free and online, making it accessible to anyone. The program includes women from all continents, socioeconomic levels, ages, and cultures.

Like the WIN members, the IWL women were an equally accomplished group coming together from all over in a way Sarah had never felt before. Again, the diversity of the women struck her, as did the program's impressive quality.

The women lead very different lives, yet we have so much in common. Sarah says, "So even though you're from a different country, speak different languages, and live in contrasting circumstances, cultures, and expectations, the battles and struggles are universal."

Bonnie has a specific process for matching mentor pairs instead of the traditional dyads. Sometimes she uses intergenerational collaboration, where you match a younger mentor with a more experienced mentee to create a substantive paradigm shift.

In the program's initial phase, Sarah's mentor was 15 years younger and a human-rights and freedom activist in Kenya, Africa. Sarah says, "I learned so much from this woman, and we are still friends. We formed a profoundly deep relationship that changed our lives. Additionally, as a result of our relationship, it has changed the lives of the people from my mentor's world."

Sarah now spends some of her time doing charitable work for her mentor's organization in Kenya, which helps teenage girls attend school.

In the second six months, Sarah became a mentor. She and her mentee were juxtaposed in age and life experience. Her mentee was a gregarious Eastern European politician, ten years her senior, with flaming red hair and a personality to match. It was exciting and rewarding for both women.

Like many other first-time mentors, in the beginning, Sarah didn't believe there was any knowledge of significant value she could impart to her mentee. However, Sarah provided a safe container, and through the program's brilliance, these two opposites formed a bond, sharing very tender and honest moments of the mentee's discovery process.

Unconditional acceptance, a core element of the IWL program, creates a depth of trust, which allows the women to let their guard down, becoming vulnerable. Peeling back the protective layers, you witness your most authentic self emerge. Breakdowns reveal breakthroughs facilitated by Bonnie's incredible program.

The process used by IWL lifts these women, helps them uncover their confidence, and provides opportunities to develop a deeper level of self-awareness regarding their skills. In addition, it provides women with what they need, global connections, inclusivity, and a safe space.

One example of the impact of IWL on Sarah's courage to be authentic was at a convention in London.

Sarah represented her company and spoke on the "Future of Work." As their spokesperson, she felt the expectation to present a particular image by dressing in the typical blue and beige or neutral corporate color scheme.

Additionally, she was meeting some colleagues for the first time in person.

However, because of her IWL discoveries, Sarah challenged the perceived norms by choosing to wear a bold "non-corporate" green print dress.

While her outfit was a courageous departure from the expected and out-of-character for Sarah, she felt more authentic, empowered, and feminine in the dress.

Sarah says, "I represent the future of work. Full stop. Nothing else, no explanation, no apology."

She went from being busy and overwhelmed with no role models to being more intentional and self-confident. Today, she surrounds herself with kind, generous, optimistic, affirming, and inspiring women willing to be there for each other.

A side effect of being part of a circle of powerful women is what she calls "recurring magic; it empowers and nourishes the soul."

"I now realize that the WIN conference in Rome, and then two years later finding Bonnie's business card, were the steppingstones for me to be me. I saw something different at the conference and again in Bonnie and IWL that I had never seen before – and it pulled me in," says Sarah.

IWL finds you when you're ready to be your authentic feminine self.

"The program is how I found my way to me."

While she's involved with quite a few organizations, all doing good work, none compare to Sarah's experience with Inspired Women Lead.

Sarah says, "I have no words to describe this program; none of the other programs have given me the same depth of learning or the same exposure." At IWL, you find your people and yourself.

Chapter 19

What's Next

The next chapter for Bonnie Fatio

> "We do not pass the torch on to another; we use it to light the flames of others."

We're continuously evolving and stretching, and our view of ourselves and the impact we can have on the world is constantly transforming.

I am blessed by the extraordinary experiences and people I've met. My journey continues as I have more to do and more people to reach, ultimately as many lives as people living on Earth.

Looking ahead, I see two paths into the future that run partly parallel yet will often merge. One relates specifically to Inspired Women Lead, and the other is my personal or professional path.

On the personal side, a highlight will be playing "Auntie

Mame" to my three grandchildren, traveling more widely with them to explore other cultures they have only dreamed or read about. I will enjoy spending extra time with them during their formative years as they develop their opinions of the world.

Professionally, I plan to accept more paid speaking engagements. I love public speaking, relating to audiences, the challenge of inspiring action, and the travel associated with diverse events.

Rather than the what's-in-it-for-me-today mentality, the world is crying out for a new form of leadership: one that is more fair, peaceful, inclusive, and concerned for the future of our planet. With my extensive leadership experience, years of training women leaders around the globe, and my broad research, I am excited to share two new speech topics that are trending in today's business and political arenas:

- ***The UnWorthiness Gene: Beyond the Imposter Syndrome***
- ***Breaking Out of the Male Box***

Although designed for women, my speeches benefit all leaders. We need a new model for women and men: authentic leadership driven by values and vision. Often when I enter conversations with men, they comment, "That's what we want too, to be able to be genuine."

The future will also see me speaking on *1 + 1 = Exponential.* Whether we lead in our family, community, company, country, or the world, as women, we have more significant influence than we know. We create the butterfly effect. Just as a butterfly fluttering its wings in Brazil can cause a hurricane in North America, so too can we have an outreach that extends far beyond our imagination, touching as many lives as people on Earth.

I plan to write additional books following this second one, the first being *AgeEsteem®: Growing A Positive Attitude Toward Aging.*

As a visionary, I knew that IWL would need to thrive without me. So now, the time has come to move toward stepping down from the Presidency and day-to-day operations of Inspired Women Lead and create a Board of Advisors to help steer IWL into the future.

Removing myself from my current role will enable me to continue the work of IWL on a more grass-roots level. One example is reaching women in underserved regions who may not speak English and balancing that with the unique richness of the program that bridges women among different cultures using English as the basis. I would like to test at least one prototype for such a program in a second language that extends over several countries.

Lastly, I often think how wonderful it would be to just lie in a hammock and do nothing. In fact, I do take breaks among the trees to replenish my soul and mind. I love these spiritual moments of peace and reflection. Doing a bit more of it would be pleasant, and who knows where my thoughts might lead me.

The next chapter for Inspired Women Lead

This book has honored our history and legacy as we marked our milestones and accomplishments.

In 2022, two sizeable undertakings were positively influencing our future. First, the launch of our Alumnae Community opening meaningful opportunities for our IWL alumnae to remain connected. Second, a task force reviewed our branding to keep us relevant, commencing with a new logo and website.

To fuel our momentum towards the next stage in our development, now is the time to inject a more business approach into Inspired Women Lead while keeping its collaborative, value-driven leadership style with a Council of equals focused on our vision.

Volunteers remain crucial, and opportunities within IWL offer a safe environment to develop their leadership further. However, volunteers are no longer enough to continuously grow IWL. As we move forward, we will seek a mix of volunteers and paid staff to ensure the unique quality of our program and the tangible benefits it brings to the women and their work environments.

We have attracted women from major global companies like Skyguide, UNICEF, and Velocity Global, that focus on advancing women within their organizations. We are ready to attract more companies as sponsors and partners in our quest to positively transform the world, one woman at a time. We accept that to achieve our vision, we cannot do it alone.

The timing is also auspicious to create an Advisory Council composed of exemplary women leaders from various disciplines and different regions of the world, providing greater perspective, exposure, and a focus on funding.

The future will be decided and planned by our IWL leaders.

Members of the Executive Council will be a constant catalyst to move IWL into the future.

Each has proven herself in multiple ways as a leader and brings a unique set of expertise to complement each of the others.

The IWL vision of a world of peace, understanding, and collaboration, where each individual is valued and respected for her or his uniqueness, will be realized when authentic feminine leadership sweeps the world.

The next chapter for the Case Study Subjects

Daeyoung Kim
For many Koreans, conversational English is a significant barrier to international experiences. With Bonnie's blessing and cooperation, Daeyoung is developing a version of the IWL mentor training program in Korean with the hope of sharing the themes within South Korea.

In the meantime, throughout this year, Daeyoung and a colleague in partnership with the National YWCA of Korea are hosting a monthly lecture series to promote female leadership. Non-Koreans may be unaware of the barriers for women in South Korea, and Daeyoung has her sights set on closing the gap. She's working on a lineup of speakers from several promising NGO activists, business leaders, and entrepreneurs.

Renee van der Burg

Through her company, Capricorn HR Consulting, Renée continues to work with individuals looking to step into their full potential in their careers and personal lives. She carries the unconditional acceptance for others and authentic leadership she learned at IWL while working with people to develop resilience and identify coping strategies. In this way, Renée says she's a sparring partner for those who need an external, neutral, knowledgeable corporate advisor.

Andrea Delannoy

Her ultimate plan is to integrate the MOD-ELLE program into every school in Switzerland.

To her surprise, she's now considered a gender expert and sought out by newspapers for interviews and other organizations for presentations.

She's also making a difference for the Swiss in her new opinions and issues column published in 24heures newspaper that's read countrywide. She's thrilled that they approached her with this extraordinary opportunity.

Josephine Ndirias

Josephine will continue to help women through education, access to healthcare, freedom of choice, and realizing they have a voice and have been silent long enough.

Her organization, Mukogodo Girls Empowerment Programme, is currently fundraising with the intent to build a community resource center. It will be a place to hold holiday workshops, ongoing mentoring, and host cultural celebrations.

Because food insecurity is another grave concern, addressing hunger issues is also at the top of her priority list. Maasai women have a natural talent for beading and earning from their artisan craft; however, marketing is a challenge. To assist them in becoming independent and financially self-sufficient, they help the artists diversify their products. For example, some are learning to make soaps from available materials in addition to beaded goods.

Sarah Fern

Sarah loves IWL, believes the program needs a legacy and does her part to ensure its longevity. When she meets women who exhibit a "fire in their belly" attitude, she recommends them to IWL.

Her recommendations help other women uncover their confidence and develop a deeper self-awareness regarding their skills.

Sarah's not actively scouting out women; instead, she's keenly observant and quickly identifies those who would be a good fit. She doesn't do it for any recognition or compensation, instead, she does it for the pure joy of seeing another woman come into her own.

You have seen what steps each of us has and is taking to change the world ... I invite you to explore your next steps.

One woman can change the world.

Are you that woman?

Contact me so I may support your journey.
bonnie@afireinherbelly.com

Receive regular emails with *inspirational* **messages from Bonnie to boost your confidence**

Complete your details on the link below!

afireinherbelly.com/inspiration

www.ingramcontent.com/pod-product-compliance
Lightning Source LLC
Chambersburg PA
CBHW071459080526
44587CB00014B/2154